RAA, PAA TET; The Power to Motivate People

Building your Team through RAA, PAA, TET. The Playbook for Success

Charles Tatum

with Craig Pifer

© 2019 Copyright

Text copyright reserved by Charles Tatum and Table Island, LLC

RAA, PAA, TET™ is a trademark of Table Island, LLC. All rights reserved.

The contents of this book may not be reproduced, duplicated or transmitted in any form or by any means without direct written permission from the author.

Table of Contents

Foreword

An Introduction

TI VUM

Planning

Team Dynamics

Process Dynamics

The Contract

Power – Responsibility, Accountability, Authority

Motivation – Power, Achievement, Affiliation

People – Talent, Experience, Technique

Applying the *"I"* – Taking the Initiative

Finally, bringing it all together

An added Bonus, COIL

Reference Summary Table

Graphical Summary

Gray Hairs and Closure

Appendix A – Templates and Examples

Appendix B – References

This book is dedicated to our family members, past and present who have influenced and inspired us the most in our lives.

This book is also dedicated to the motivational experts that have come before us. Without their leadership, influence and extensive knowledge in human motivation, other motivational topics and the workplace we never would have been able to complete this book.

"Thank You"

We will open this book with some great quotes to get you started.

"If it's a good idea, go ahead and do it. It's much easier to apologize than it is to get permission" – Rear Admiral Grace Hopper

"You'll always miss 100% of the shots you don't take" – Wayne Gretzky

"Never let the fear of striking out get in your way" – Babe Ruth

"Energy and persistence conquer all things" – Benjamin Franklin

"The secret of getting ahead is getting started" – Mark Twain

"Goals not written down are just dreams" – Emmitt Smith

"If you can dream it, you can do it" – Walt Disney

"Dream big, start small. But most of all, start" – Simon Sinek

"Live the dream, have fun, enjoy your life" – Jesse Ventura

"Make a difference. Be a positive influence and role model"

Foreword

Every motivational book you buy is different in one way or another. Some books provide examples for how their motivational principles provide you results based on extensive research studies. Other books tell a story on how their motivational principles helped to change the way teams, companies and institutions operate for the better. My book RAA, PAA, TET; The Power to Motivate People could fit into both of these structures, but I decided to keep the book short and to the point to emphasize the key motivational principles I have learned over the years.

The RAA, PAA, TET motivational principles as defined in this book can fit into a lot of different team-based environments and applications. This includes sports, institutional and business teams. It took me some time to figure out how to "fit together" the RAA, PAA TET motivational principles and how they fit into the different team-based environments and applications. I have made every effort to show you how RAA, PAA, TET fits into these environments.

I also provide you examples and templates you can use in a business-application environment. In the subject title areas of this book which I explain in the introduction chapter, I have called out the specific business-applications you can use to make your business environment-based team better. Where they apply, use them. They can help improve how your team operates.

In my development of RAA, PAA, TET; Power and RAA is the first motivational principle, which I learned while I was in the US Army. Motivation and PAA came second which I learned through David McClelland and his book *Human Motivation*. And finally, People and TET came last which I learned through my experiences in the military and afterwards in the corporate world.

At first, I had never planned on writing about RAA, PAA, TET and the Power to Motivate People. It was something I always planned to keep to myself, in my own journals, to ensure what I brought to the teams I was on or leading, I was able to provide key value-added steps for their success. Even though I learned the RAA, PAA, TET motivational principle years ago. Once I decided to write about RAA, PAA, TET, through the motivation of others, it also took me some time to figure out how to truly fit the motivation principles together into a book that is easy to read. With this book, the time to introduce you to RAA, PAA, TET; The Power to Motivate People is now. I hope you enjoy this book as much as I have enjoyed writing it along with the help I received from my friends, particularly Craig Pifer when writing it.

Thanks and enjoy,

Charles

An Introduction

This book does not introduce anything new. It does emphasize motivational principles that are proven and have been in use for a very long time. This book takes these established principles and combines them in a manner that makes them easy to understand and follow for improving your team's performance along with improving your own personal performance. Some of these principles come from industry frameworks for their industry best practices. One example of this comes from the American Society for Quality, ASQ and their quality management principles which we cover towards the end of this book.

Also, with the expansion of social media there is a lot of information available on-line in leading and improving your team and yourself. This information comes in the form of articles and blogs along with Twitter, Facebook and LinkedIn messages, talking about how we can improve our working relationships and what we can do to better ourselves to become a better leader and a better team player. As an example, General Colin Powell was once quoted as saying: "Leadership is all about people. It is not about organizations. It is not about plans. It is not about strategies. It is all about people motivating people to get the job done. You have to be people-centered." Another example comes from Jack and Suzy Welch and their own definition of leadership. To summarize their leadership definition, the five essential traits to leadership are:

- Positive energy.
- Ability to energize others.
- Ability to make tough calls (decision making).
- Having the talent to execute.
- Passion.

Leadership definitions can also be found from the places you visit. An example of this comes from the General George S. Patton Museum at Ft. Knox, Ky where there is the question: What is leadership? The answer is simple: "Leadership is influencing people by providing purpose, direction and motivation."

As you read this book, you will find that the RAA, PAA, TET principles and the Power to Motivate People are consistent with these quotes along with the other quotes and reference citations we have included in this book.

Again, with the expansion of social media there is also a lot of information available coming from the happy employee and the not-so-happy or disgruntled / disengaged employee. An example of this is what you see on Glassdoor.com. Glassdoor's website is great for providing you details on how current and past employees feel about their current or former employer through their reviews of the company or institution they work for or have worked for. This book is written to:

- Deal with and in some aspects, compliment some of the current articles you see and to create an easy-to-remember acronym that has a "flow" to it for addressing the challenges you may face when leading a team.
- Help you address the disgruntled or the "disengaged" team member and how you can make them active participants in the success of your team.
- Present you a way for building a team you will be proud to lead and creates the right environment where your team members go from being disengaged to being fully engaged.
- Take into account the rapid business and technological changes that are occurring in today's world.
- Provide you a framework which you can build your team from for dealing with these rapid changes.
- Provide you key power motivational leadership principles to make your team fundamentally sound.
- Act as a playbook for your team to follow.
- Help you LEAD!

This book's information is presented from a leader's perspective. This does not mean that you cannot take these principles and use them for self-directed or personal improvement. You can.

To help you understand how the principles presented in this book relate to what you can do for your team, sports analogies for golf, soccer, football and baseball teams are used to help you visualize and understand when it comes to leading your team, fitting in with your team and what your interaction within your team can and should be.

As we said before, most of the principles presented in this book have existed for some time. They have been published in various forms and dissected by the experts for many years and with great success. Through a combination of key principles, a "simple" set of easy-to-remember acronyms have been created for you to apply when leading your team. When the principles of this book are combined with other well-known acronyms and principles, the final outcome from this book will improve your ability to lead your team to greater success by:

- You taking the initiative for empowering your people.
- Delivering positive motivation to your team.
- Bringing together the right people to the right job.

Through this, your team can understand and follow your new team philosophy to become the team you want them to be. A fundamentally sound team.

Great Leaders and the Fundamentals

Great teams are led by great leaders on and off the field of play. Great leaders or coaches from the past like Vince Lombardi, Chuck Noll and John Wooden brought with them a certain team philosophy that stressed the importance of commitment, fundamentals and attention to detail. As an example, Vince Lombardi, the coaching legend of the Green Bay Packers taught his team how individual commitment impacts your team and your community. Coach Lombardi said: "Individual commitment to a group effort – that is what makes a team work, a company work, a society work, a civilization work." Chuck Noll, the coaching legend of the Pittsburgh Steelers, taught his team how to deal with the unexpected. Coach Noll said: "When dealing with the unexpected, know and follow the fundamentals." And finally, John Wooden, the coaching legend of the UCLA Bruins, taught his team the importance in the attention to detail when it comes to the team. Coach Wooden said: "It's the little details that are vital. Little things make big things happen." These great coaches through their leadership and fundamental teachings defined the core competencies their teams needed for them to be successful on the playing field or court. By applying the principles that are presented to you in this book, you, yourself can become the ultimate leader for your team to follow, hopefully no different than a Vince Lombardi, a Chuck Noll or a John Wooden.

With the foundational building blocks that are provided to you in this book, you can make a statement that will resonate throughout your team and provide them the fundamentals needed for their success. Once you and your team get use to these fundamental principles and their application, you and your team can achieve success that can continue to motivate your team to even greater successes and can also motivate others to want to become a member of your successful team. And when we think about the fundamentals and principles, it is important to know that they are inter-related and bring value. Stephen Covey said: "Principles are guidelines for human conduct that are proven to have enduring, permanent value. They are fundamental."

As shown above and contained throughout this book are important "quotes and phrases" that you will want to remember which come from some outstanding authors and leaders. These quotes and phrases are important when it comes to the principles you will learn when reading this book. Title areas and topics of special importance are also in **<u>Bold and Underlined</u>** print to stress their particular importance in this book. Where it applies to business, the term "A Business Application" has also been added to the underlined title area.

The flow of this book's information and the steps you can take has been organized to assist you as you progress from start to finish when you apply the new knowledge you will learn. This includes the planning process steps needed for defining your team and your team process. The actual steps you can take for building your team through RAA, PAA, TET along with any process improvement initiatives you can take on after you have successfully built your team.

At the end of this book you are also provided templates and examples that you can use when you start building your team. Now, the main purpose of this book is for you and your team to follow the RAA, PAA, TET principles for building your team. If you have your own team building templates that you prefer to use over the ones provided to you in this book, please feel free to do so.

The RAA, PAA, TET principles presented to you in this book can result in long term ROI results for you and your team if you take the initiative to learn them and apply them. For your "investment" strategies, John C. Maxwell said: "If you want to lead to the full extent of your potential, you need to invest in your people." Invest in your people on your team. They are your most important commodity, your most valuable asset. Put in place the resources needed for this investment in developing your people, your team, to be the best they can be.

Building your team through RAA, PAA, TET

Previously, it was mentioned there would be a number of "simple" acronyms for you to learn and follow. The main starting point of these acronyms is *PMPI*. This will be the lead acronym for the other acronyms which follow. When you start building your team through RAA, PAA, TET you are taking the initiative to building an outstanding team.

Power and RAA

The first capital letter "P" of the lead acronym *PMPI*, represents Power. Not power in the traditional sense, but principles, concepts and tools you can use and introduce to your team to better empower your people. Power is the first part of your foundation building blocks, "RAA." RAA stands for Responsibility, Accountability and Authority.

Motivation and PAA

The second capital letter of the lead acronym *PMPI*, "M", stands for Motivation. There are some amazing books written on motivation by some outstanding experts in the field. It is highly recommended that you take the time to read some of them as this book will utilize a number of their motivational concepts to stress the importance of team motivation.

One of these motivational experts is David McClelland. David was an expert in the area of human motivation. It is through his work on Power, Achievement and Affiliation that the next building block is created. Through Motivation, comes the second part of your foundation building blocks, "PAA." PAA stands for Power, Achievement and Affiliation.

People and TET

The last capital letter "P" of the lead acronym *PMPI* is probably the most important and represents People. As we said before, People are the backbone of your team, your greatest asset. Treat them well. Your people are the most important attribute for you and your team's success. Through People, comes the last part of your foundation building blocks, "TET." TET stands for Talent, Experience and Technique.

Before each section where *PMPI* and RAA, PAA, TET are defined, formal definitions are provided from the Merriam-Webster's dictionary. These definitions provide you a recognized standard reference for these terms. When you combine these acronyms with another powerful acronym SMART (Specific, Measurable, Attainable, Realistic and Timely) along with using the team dynamic principles (Forming, Storming, Norming and Performing), you create a strong set of tools for the building of your team. The application of these key acronyms and principles provides you with the tools and techniques that you can use for successfully building and leading fully dynamic teams.

Taking the Initiative

After learning these principles, it will be up to you to take the lead and the initiative to apply them. Through this initiative you close the loop for the lead acronym *PMPI,* by applying the *"I"* when it comes to building your team. Applying the *"I"* and taking the initiative puts in motion the steps you want to take on for building your team through RAA, PAA, TET.

And finally, the RAA, PAA, TET principles can apply to any type of team you will lead. And when we talk about the team within the context of this book, the word team is synonymous with any type of institution, company, organization or department; large or small. For organizations larger than your team, the term "institution" will apply within the contents of this book. So, whether it is on the football grid iron, a basketball court, or a baseball diamond; whether it is in the classroom, the stateroom, the boardroom, the conference room or the work floor, all teams can benefit from building your team through RAA, PAA, TET along with the principles for which it provides.

TI VUM

TI VUM	• Take the Initiative • Have a Vision • Basic to Thorough Understanding of the Essentials, the Fundamentals • Move and Motivate (Move on IT)

Before you start the planning for the building of your team through RAA, PAA, TET; defining your team process or playbook, think about what you can do to ensure that you and your team will be successful from a leadership standpoint. You start by thinking about and looking at the big picture, the team vision for your team. You will define and document the strategic (leadership) and tactical (management) approach you will take when it comes to the big picture. Many times, your team's big picture is reacting to:

- Changing market conditions.
- New customer requirements or deliverables; new business requirements or competitive pressures.
- Legal situations or regulatory compliance.

When defining the big picture, you must also become better at:

- Anticipation (having the vision, being "Ready Alert").
- Adaptation (the ability to respond rapidly, or "Rapid Response") when reacting to new or changing requirements.

Your ability to handle the "Anticipation and Adaptation" when it comes to the big picture comes from and requires a creative and innovative way of thinking. This type of "creative and innovative way of thinking" also assists you in creating the vision for building your team through RAA, PAA, TET. To support the creation of this vision, the first acronym TI VUM is applied to address your team's vision. TI VUM can help define your strategic approach, the basic principles for your strategic short-term and long-term initiatives and the tactical actions required to successfully execute your strategic plans. TI VUM is:

- TI – Taking the Initiative.
- V – Having a Vision, being a Visionary.
- U – Having a basic to thorough Understanding of team essentials, fundamentals and principles for your team, your team's mission and your team's purpose.
- M – Moving in the right direction and being Motivated to getting it done.

TI – Taking the Initiative

H.G. Wells said: "He that does not contemplate the future is destined to be overwhelmed by it." William Jennings Bryan said: "Destiny is not by chance, but by choice." And President Abraham Lincoln and Peter Drucker both said: "The best way to predict your future is to create it." Taking the initiative is taking control of your own destiny, your own future along with your team's destiny, your team's future. When you take the initiative, you are grabbing the bull by the horns and taking control of what you want to accomplish, an outstanding team through well-thought-out strategic planning. By taking the initiative, you are setting in motion the steps needed for building your team through RAA, PAA, TET. These steps provide you a foundational framework, the building blocks for taking the initiative for the plans and execution you can follow when building your team. As said before, apply TI VUM for defining, building and tackling the strategic planning along with executing the tactical planning for your team.

V – Having a Vision, being a Visionary

When you look at the vision, the big picture for your team, you, as a leader will define what you want and expect from your team. Jeff Bezos once said: "Unrealistic beliefs on scope – often hidden and undiscussed – kill high standards." For the big picture, you will:

- Define the purpose, the goals and the scope for your team.
- Engage your team and get their feedback when it comes to the big picture, your team's vision.
- Be creative and innovative when it comes to your team's vision.

Stephen Covey's Habit 2 states: "Begin with the end in mind. All things are created twice; first mentally, then physically. The key to creativity is to begin with the end in mind, with a vision and a blue print of a desired result." When it comes to your team, the end or desired result you are looking for is a highly effective team along with a vision that inspires your team to move people in the right direction. When it comes to your vision, once again, remember, "Destiny is not by chance, but by choice." It is up to you and your team to determine the destiny, to create the future for your team based on the vision which has been set for them. You will determine your team's vision by the direction you want your team to take, your team roadmap, along with any key decisions associated with that roadmap. Another simple way of looking at your team vision comes from the movie *Caddy Shack*. Ty, one of the country club's best golfers, tells the young ambitious caddy, Danny, who is interested in attending college to "See your future, be your future." Look to the future for your team's success and survival. BE YOUR FUTURE AND MAKE YOUR TEAM SURVIVAL MANDATORY. And when it comes to looking into the future, you must be able to predict the behavior of your customer and your competitors in order to survive. Know that change can occur, especially in today's dynamic work environment and when your customer's or your competitor's behavior changes, you and your team must change with it.

Professional Golfer Justin Thomas in an article by Golf Digest magazine said: "See it, then hit it. You can't waver during crunch time." For your team's vision, you and your team will need to consider where you want your team to be in the near and distant futures, then go out and do it. Don't just expect it to happen because of past results and don't just look at it in terms of days or months. Tony Robbins said: "Setting goals is the first step in turning the invisible into the visible." Set the strategic goals for your team and use the principles of RAA, PAA, TET to "visually" get you there. Success comes from meeting realistic goals and expectations. Make sure the goals which have been set for your team are high, but realistic. Unrealistic goals can lead to an overworked team that makes mistakes over and over that requires re-work as they work hard trying to meet your unrealistic expectations.

You will have two strategic plans in place, a short-term strategic plan and a long-term strategic plan. Your short-term strategic planning is what you want your team to accomplish over the next year, to 3 years out and should be based on a monthly review schedule for the first 2 years and a quarterly based review schedule for year 3. Long-term strategic planning will cover anything 3 to 5 years out and should be based on a quarterly based review schedule for years 3 and 4 and an annual review schedule for year 5. And as each year progresses, you can adjust your short-term and long-term strategic initiatives to address any change your team may experience.

If you ever watch professional golf, the really good professional golfers visualize each golf shot they take. This visualization is part of their tactical plan or approach for the round they are playing at that moment in time. They picture their back swing, the downward motion of their swing, the striking of the ball and its outcome based on their visualization. Their golf swing mechanics is a consistent and repeatable process, through what some people would call muscle memory. And when they do make a shot not to their liking, they will look at their swing mechanics very briefly and make the minor adjustments in their swing mechanics needed for the next time they stand over the ball and prepare for their next shot. Before they get to this point, the really good top professional golfers will have a strategic plan of what they want to accomplish for the year long before the golf season even begins. They will have a team of coaches and consultants working with them to plan for the upcoming season and beyond. As an example, when Professional Golfer Kyle Stanley won the 2017 Quicken Loans National golf tournament, during Kyle's victory interview he was asked what it took for him to win. His response included working with his team of family members and coaches and his focus on the process which his team put in place to allow him to reach the victory podium.

In comparison, the strategic and tactical planning for your team is no different. Use the experts inside and outside of your team to help you define your team vision and to visualize the big picture, to "See your future." Visualize frame-by-frame, shot-by-shot, round-by-round, season-by-season years 1-3 in your short-term strategic planning and then execute on it through your short-term tactical plan.

Visualize frame-by-frame, shot-by-shot, round-by-round, season-by-season, years 3-5 in your long-term strategic planning and then execute on it through your long-term tactical plan. As they say in the NBC RBC commercial for the PGA RBC Canadian Open, "When you have the right people behind you, there is no limit to how far you can go."

For long-term planning, Peter Drucker said: "Long-range planning does not deal with future decisions, but with the future of present decisions." Peter went on to say: "What gets measured gets improved." For your strategic planning:

- Document your short-term and long-term strategic initiatives / plans.
- Communicate to everyone what your strategic plans are for your team.
- Have a team motto or team mission statement and team principles that are based on your vision.
- Make sure that everyone is on-board and ready to execute your strategic plans.
- Set-up key performance measurements that provide value (also referred to as KPIs, (key performance indicators)), then modify and take action when improvements are needed to your strategic plans.
- Don't overlook the obvious. The key item for your mission success can be right under your nose. You just have to look to find it.

U – Having a Basic to Thorough Understanding

Stephen Covey said: "To begin with the end in mind means to start with a clear understanding of your destination. It means to know where you're going so that you better understand where you are now and so that the steps you take are always in the right direction." Move your team in the right direction and understand what it takes to get you there.

- Start out by having a basic understanding of your team along with their respective mission and their purpose.
- Have a basic understanding of the team essentials and how they apply to your team, the team mission and your team's purpose.
- Use the Essential Elements of Information (EEI) of Who, What, Where, When, How and Why for defining these team essentials.
- Communicate these EEI-based team essentials to your team.
- Use the feedback you receive from your team to allow you to gain a thorough understanding of your team, their team mission and their purpose.
- Your basic understanding will then lead to a thorough understanding of your team.

- Your thorough understanding of the team essentials will lead to a thorough understanding of the fundamental principles you will need for your team.
- Having a thorough understanding is knowing the fundamental principles for building a successful team and then knowing how to apply the fundamental principles to your team.

Building your team through RAA, PAA, TET will provide you these fundamental principles.

- The basic and thorough understanding of your team will lead to a mutual understanding and a shared common goal for your team.
- This will create a team community, a "team culture" with shared cultural norms that everyone on your team can associate with and belong to.

A great example of this comes from the video game *Madden 11* from EA Sports. In the video game there is an introductory piece by Drew Brees, the quarterback for the New Orleans Saints. In his introduction, Drew asks "What does it take to win?" Drew's answer is simple: "Teammates focused on the same goal, fighting for the city they call home. Goals made through the confidence, the skill and the strength of the team along with the city (their community) which they support." John C. Maxwell said: "The bottom line is that the invitation to lead people is an invitation to make a difference. Good leadership changes individual lives. It forms teams. It builds organizations. It impacts communities."

- Understand the goals which have been set for your team and how they fit within your team culture.
- Get to know your people on your team within your shared community.
- Know that your people are your team's greatest asset, the key resource to your team's success.
- Know your team inside and out along with what your team can accomplish.
- Thoroughly knowing your team can support your team's tactical plan and initiatives. In turn, this can support the execution of the overall strategic plan, initiative and vision.
- Follow the principles for team dynamics, process dynamics and RAA, PAA, TET for executing your tactical plan to make your team

better prepared for your short-term and long-term strategic plans and goals.
- And finally, have a thorough understanding of your competition to allow you to have a plan of attack when it comes to meeting the face-to-face challenge from your competition and beating them on the field of play or in the arena.

M – Moving in the right direction and being Motivated

Will Rogers said: "Even if you are on the right track, you will get run over if you just sit there." Don't just sit there. Follow through on your strategic and tactical plans and move on it. "Be your future." Henry Ford said: "Vision without execution is just hallucination." Execute your plans. Don't let your plans sit there collecting dust. Put in motion the steps needed to make your team better and more successful. Unexecuted plans do nothing for you or your team. Follow the RAA, PAA, TET principles to get the ball rolling for making you and your team more successful. And when it comes to your team's success, John C. Maxwell said: "Every time you increase the leadership ability of a person in the organization, you increase the ability of the organization to fulfill its vision."

Reverse Engineering of TI VUM (MUV IT)

Now that you are moving on your strategic and tactical initiatives, you will look to put your competition into the rear-view mirror. Adopt the motto: "It always is better to pass by your competition than to being the one getting passed." Always be the one taking the initiative, inspiring your team, moving forward and looking back on the competition instead of not moving forward and looking back at yourself wondering why the competition was able to pass you by.

Now that you are taking the initiative, inspiring your team and moving forward with TI VUM, you are at the stage where you will apply "MUV IT" (forward) within your team. You may think this step in the process is hokey or redundant, but there is a reason to do "IT". Now that we are "MUVing IT" through TI VUM, we are moving "IT" by using the latest tools to support your team. These tools come in the form of Information Technology, or IT.

Purchase and use the best IT tools available in computer software and applications, computers, laptops, tablets, printers, scanners, fax machines, smart phones and other IT peripherals you can find to make your team faster and better at what they do. IT tools complement the team and better serve the customer, internally and externally. They help improve your team's plan, execution and efficiency. No different than making an investment in your people, make an investment in the IT tools they use. Don't just look at IT as being an expense, but as a valuable asset to your team, no different than how you look at your people, your most valuable asset.

Integrate – A Business Application

Integrate across your institution, your IT processes, tools and people into all your other institutional business functions. Integrate across your institution, all your team processes. This includes, your Sales and Marketing, Regulatory, Legal, Operations, Purchasing, Procurement, Supply Chain, Maintenance, Billing and IT team processes. Take the initiative, inspire and move your team forward to the next higher level in the business food chain. Don't settle for second best and use RAA, PAA, TET; The Power to Motivate People to get you there executing the vision which has been set forth for your team.

Planning

Planning	• Taking the Initiative, Planning, Executing, Tracking Progress, Finalizing and Approving

Before building your team through RAA, PAA, TET, you need to do some initial planning.

- You start by creating a project charter to define the high-level project objectives and expectations for the building of your team.
- This is followed by business requirements for drilling down and getting to the next level of detail for the project objectives and expectations which you first defined in your project charter.
- From there, you will need to have a plan of attack for your project. This is the planning you will do for the building of your team.

Sun Tzu said: "Every battle is won before it is ever fought." This battle requires thorough and effective planning. Think of and prepare for every possible scenario, real (has happened before in the past and will most likely happen again in the future) or imaginary (has the potential of happening in the future). Understand your team's mission along with the goals, objectives and expectations that have been set for you and your team when you go through your planning exercise. The team dynamics, process dynamics and building your team through RAA, PAA, TET principles as defined in this book will help you complete your planning exercise.

When planning the building of your team, make sure you cover the triple constraints of project management. They are quality, cost and delivery. In addition to the triple constraints, you must know concisely what is in-scope and out-of-scope for the work your team is expected to deliver in order to build a successful team. Building your team through RAA, PAA, TET can assist you in delivering a quality product.

The second component for delivering a quality product is controlling your costs. This will include your IT purchases and any team training that may be required to improve the team's performance. Understand what the cost components of your project will be and only include the cost components that can bring value to you and your team. The third component is the time it takes to deliver a quality product. The delivery or time required for your team building is determined by you and your team. The key for success is to ensure that you take the proper amount of time to build and prepare your team. Proper and effective planning:

- Can lead to a well-executed plan.
- Helps remove the potential fire drills and the "crisis modes" that can occur during plan execution.
- Reduces the number of risks and issues that can occur when you start executing your plan.

Appendix A of this book includes some excellent project and quality management tools you can use to complete your planning phase.

Benjamin Franklin said: "Those that fail to plan, plan to fail." In this section, you will be presented a proven plan of attack, one that you will apply to complete this planning initiative. Tools to use for this planning initiative include being SMART, using EEI and a series of Why questions, or "The 5 Whys" (drill down) type of question and answer session for starting the planning process. The steps for applying SMART, EEI and The 5 Whys will be defined in the later sections of this book and should be used when defining the planning steps, you will take for the building of your team. There are certain fundamental planning steps that need to be followed for your team building initiative. The first step is taking the initiative.

Taking the Initiative

When you initiate your team building project, you will:

- Define the purpose for building your team through RAA, PAA, TET.

- Define the objectives and expectations for your team building along with any reasons that may hinder you from completing this task.
- Look to the past while planning for your team's future by referencing any past information your institution may have available that can bring value to your team building project. This includes any team process documents (AS-IS processes), team mission statements, team charters, business processes and standard operating procedures or principles (SOP) your institution may possess for the building of your team.
- Understand your institution's culture and organizational structure. This can help you when it comes to communicating the approach you and your team will take for your team building project.

Once you have gathered your historical information. Once you understand your institutional culture, the project initiative is kicked off by delivering the project charter and business requirements to your team. From there you are ready to move into the planning phase for building your team.

Planning

Louis Pasteur said: "Fortune favors the prepared mind." Chef Jose Andres in the *60 Minutes episode, Feeding Puerto Rico* said: "There has to be a plan and someone has to be responsible for that plan." Planning is the most important project phase when it comes to your team building project. And when it comes to planning, there are 3 planning categories to focus on: Strategic, Tactical and Operational (day-to-day). In the planning phase you will focus on:

- The category you are planning for.
- And take responsibility for the plan.
- And enter this planning endeavor being extremely prepared.
- Your mission when creating your plan. That mission is building your team through RAA, PAA, TET.

- And gather inputs and feedback from key team members when it comes to your mission, your project objectives and expectations.

There are key planning steps you can follow and execute when planning your RAA, PAA, TET project initiative. The key planning steps are:

- Identifying your project team stakeholders.
- Completing your project charter and business requirements.
- Completing your project Work Breakdown Structure (WBS).
- Estimating your project resource requirements for people (roles and responsibilities), delivery (schedule) and materials (budget or cost).
- Defining your ancillary project requirements (communications, quality, risk, change, procurement, etc.).
- Taking an iterative approach for the planning of your project.
- Completing your team building project plan.
- Gaining buy-in and approval to your project plan.
- Kicking off your team building RAA, PAA, TET project initiative.

Executing

Once you have obtained your approvals and you have officially kicked off your team building project, you are now ready to execute your project plan. Your project plan and your ancillary plans will help define what you will need to do for the building of your team. In the movie *Storks*, the Storks team motto is: "Make a plan, stick to the plan, always deliver." Building your team through RAA, PAA, TET is your mission for which you will focus on when it comes to executing your plan and delivering the RAA, PAA, TET principles to your team. The execution of your plan is based on the project charter, the business requirements along with your ancillary plans that support your efforts (your communication plan, quality plan, and / or risk plan as an example).

Tracking Progress

As you execute your project activities as defined in your business requirements and your WBS, you will communicate early and often to your project team stakeholders as to the project's progress. You will also identify and address change. As you receive changes to your business requirements, communicate and gain feedback from all your project team stakeholders prior to making any change to your requirements, your budget and / or your project plan. Through your progress tracking, you are ensuring that everyone is "on the same page" and they share the same expectations when it comes to the building of your team. After communicating the changes, obtain approval for the change from the project team stakeholders. Tools that are useful for tracking progress include risk and issues logs. Create these logs to identify potential risks and known issues to the project. Risks are items that have the potential to occur but have not yet happened. When a risk is realized it converts to being an issue.

The risk and issues logs provide the capability to identify, create and execute corrective actions in a timely manner than having to wait and take the extra time and effort to create action plans to address issues without the prior knowledge of what the risk (prior to the issue) was when the risk was first recognized and introduced. These logs are also used to record information as to the "lessons learned" for your project. The lessons learned can be reviewed at the end of your project delivery by your project team to improve the efficiency of future projects. Lessons learned can also contribute to future best practices within your team or your institution.

Finalizing and Approving

After you have completed the business requirement and WBS activities or "the project phases" for building your team through RAA, PAA, TET, you will close the project. When closing your project, you will:

- Confirm that all the project work is complete and in accordance to the project charter, the business requirements and the WBS.

- Confirm acceptance and obtain formal approval from the project team stakeholders based on the successful delivery of these requirements.
- Document your lessons learned, positive and negative, for the things you have learned as you have progressed through the project that can bring value to your future projects.
- Index the project or process repository and archive all your project deliverables and project documentation for future use.
- Clear all external invoices, where required, and release all the project team resources from the project.
- Officially close the project.

These are the steps you can take when you start to define your team dynamics; your process dynamics; defining and applying the Power, Motivation and People processes along with taking the initiative for building your team through **RAA, PAA, TET**.

Team Dynamics

Team Dynamics	• Be SMART in your approach – Specific, Measurable, Attainable, Realistic and Timely • Forming, Storming, Norming and Performing; setting up the right fundamental team environment and culture. One of value

When working on the team dynamics, you can apply the SMART approach (Specific, Measurable, Attainable, Realistic and Timely) for getting it done. The team dynamics process is based on the following steps of Forming, Storming, Norming and Performing.

Forming

Now before you form your team which we will call the Tigers, think about this. Have you ever been to a little kid's soccer game? The kids are told to chase down, go get and kick the soccer ball. They do it with so much enthusiasm, that all of them surround the soccer ball and if they are lucky, the ball moves in one direction or another with every little kid trying so hard to get to the ball and kick it. One or two might succeed and again if they are lucky, they may actually score, but for the most part it is just a cluster of little kids trying to kick a soccer ball moving it in one direction or another. When you are first forming your team, you are bringing the teammates together for the very first time. It may not be much different than a bunch of little kids trying to learn how to play soccer for their very first time.

- There can be inconsistency, ambiguity and a certain level of uncertainty along with a lack of confidence from your team.
- They may not understand what they need to do at first.
- They may not know the team's goal or what their mission is.

This is the "Forming" of your team. Leadership is your ability to properly inspire and motivate your team by leading and guiding them to meet the goals you have set for them. Douglas Bader said: "Rules are the guidance of wise men." A prime example of team guidance and the rules for leading a team comes from the movie, *Hoosiers*, where the Coach's initial main focus is team fundamentals. Coach Norman Dale starts by teaching the fundamentals of basketball to his team, which then leads to the team having the discipline to pass the ball four times before they are allowed to shoot. This four-pass offense is intended to teach the importance of and to create a culture of team play over individual play. It is your responsibility as a leader to:

- Teach or guide your team on the fundamentals that support your team goals.
- Guide your team to understanding what their mission is and how the mission relates to the team environment and culture.
- Provide the targets for which your team will aim at and how these targets relate to your team goals.

The targets should be realistic and match the expectations set for your team based on their team mission. Michelangelo said: "The greatest danger for most of us is not that our aim is too high and we miss it, but that our aim is too low and we reach it." Bo Jackson said: "Set your goals high, and don't stop till you get there." If your goals and expectations are low or based on nothing when it comes to your team, then there is a good chance you can expect nothing in return from your team when they look to take aim at the low targets which have been set for them. Set the targets and the goals for your team where they are high, but not too low where anyone can reach them. And when it comes to targets and goals, there was an excellent article by Rocky Thurston entitled *The Epitome of Teamwork* on the importance of teamwork and setting team targets and goals. In the article, the coaches' job is to inspire and motivate their team to function at their highest level. It is then the team's responsibility to perform at the high level that has been set for them. This comes from the team's ability for possessing 4 key team member traits. The 4 key traits for an outstanding team are:

- Selflessness – A team made up of individuals who care more about their teammates and the team goals, than they do for themselves. There is sense of pride amongst the team over the ego of the individual.
- Well-balanced skills – A team where individual skills balance one another. One person's strength offsets the weakness of another. The

individual's skillsets provide a diverse point of view, opinion and knowledge for them taking on their assigned tasks.
- A common goal – A team that knows and understands their goals. Effective teamwork that is based on clear direction and mutual trust, respect and agreement.
- Team-examination – A team that doesn't settle for the norm. They constantly strive to improve communication and the processes to make progress towards their target and their goal.

In summary, as you progress through the team building process, it is your responsibility as a leader to:

- Make sure your team has the ability to hit their targets by learning good teamwork fundamentals through good active coaching.
- Take charge and clearly define your team's overall mission along with setting the goals, the guidelines and the ground rules for your team as they relate to the overall mission.
- Make sure the team continually knows how to apply these principles when it comes to your team's overall mission.
- Teach your team the importance of team communication and feedback along with how to use it. This is especially important when it comes to team process improvements.

It is also your job to show them how they fit in the grand scheme of things as it relates to your team. To do this with discipline and patience as some team members will understand with ease, while others will not. Remember Rome was not built in a day and neither will your team. When you first form your team, give them a team name (example: The Tigers) that everyone will be able to associate with. As time progresses, the team members will be able to associate with the team and each other along with what it means being a "Tiger."

Storming

As you are forming your team, you will notice that some team members will want to take on a leader's role, while others prefer to be a follower. Using the soccer team analogy again, there is one kid on the Tigers team that is overly aggressive. He is running everywhere, stealing the ball away from his opponents and sometimes, even his own teammates. Johnny, the one that is trying to take charge, could feel resentment from the other teammates as he looks to take charge and be an overly authoritative and aggressive leader for the team. Some teammates will look at Johnny and say things like, "Who does this guy think he is? Does he even know what is he doing? Where does he think he is coming from?", while other teammates will see Johnny as a leader and will get behind him and support him. This situation can create disagreements and conflicts within the team. It is your responsibility as a leader to:

- Ensure that these disagreements and conflicts do not become toxic or have a negative impact on your team (Not all conflicts are bad and some good can come from some of the conflicts as they appear).
- Recognize the good from the bad in these disagreements and conflicts and to set the team members straight.
- Ensure that positive open communication exists within your team.
- Define the guidelines and the goals for the team and let everyone know what "piece of the puzzle they own", the position they are responsible for playing when it comes to your team's execution and performance as they "Storm" the field.

This comes from the "Storming" of your team and you will be provided with the steps on how to do this in the upcoming sections of this book.

Norming

Once your team understands their goals along with their mission and the area's they are responsible and accountable for they will begin to work as a cohesive team and not a bunch of individuals "just getting together."

Now back to the Tigers. They have been under your wing for some time now. Over time, they have learned their positions, their core competencies through your good active coaching. Even little Johnny, whom if directed and coached right is probably a Captain on your team, he is a General on the field. The Tigers know how to communicate on the field of play. They have the ability to defend their goal and score when they go on the offensive. This is the "Norming" of your team to where they will be able to meet any requirement or situation that is presented to them. Your team, the Tigers, are ready for the challenge. They will take on their responsibilities head on and without confusion.

Performing

When you reach this stage in your team development, the Tigers are performing as a team where they experience team-based results and not just individual achievements. With the Tigers performing as a team, they:

- Can "hit their targets" which leads to winning consistently.
- Are performing as a cohesive unit, working towards a shared common goal and understanding.
- Are part of a team. Part of a community.
- Openly communicate and they know that positive feedback is an integral part of this communication.

This is the final stage of your team dynamics, "Performing." The Tigers have been through the team dynamics. The Tigers:

- Are performing at optimal levels and meeting the expectations that you have set for them. On the field of play, the Tigers are playing their position not missing a beat and clearly running on all cylinders.
- Have become a "creature of habit" when it comes to them playing their position.
- Have been taught the fundamentals and what they need to do to play their position.
- Know how to properly support their teammates as the game progresses.
- Have the ability to handle the various situations and scenarios they will experience.
- Know how to handle and deal with adversity.
- Are empowered to succeed.
- Trust each other through teamwork, open communication and mutual respect.
- Know what it means to be part of a team, to be part of a community.
- Are reliable and every member on the team knows that they can rely on their teammates to getting the job done.

The character traits listed above are the same character traits Joe Maddon, the Manager of the Chicago Cubs expects from his players. Joe Maddon looks for players that embrace the pressure of winning along with the expectations that come with winning big.

Steve Jobs once stressed the importance of empowerment, trust and teamwork, key elements to Apple's success. Simon Sinek said: "A team is not a group of people that work together. A team is a group of people that trust each other." Stephen Covey said: "If there is little or no trust, there is no foundation for permanent success. Integrity and honesty creates the foundation of trust which is essential to cooperation and long-term personal and interpersonal growth." And finally, Patrick Lencioni said: "Trust is the foundation of real teamwork." When you empower your people, you are entrusting them to getting things done through teamwork.

Now that your team is winning, it does not mean that they are perfect. As they say in the NFL, "On any given Sunday, even the best team can lose." Let's set some stretch goals and records for your team. These team and individual records can bring great value to your team members as some of them will want to have their accomplishments enshrined. Let's recognize and reward them for their accomplishments which helps keep them on the winning side of things. As they say in a Geico Insurance commercial: "Greatness deserves recognition." Some, if not most of your team members will train harder and work harder to reach the pinnacle where they are consistently recognized and rewarded.

Team Dynamics Summary

Now that you have your team in place via Forming and Storming, you will begin teaching your team the fundamental principles for building your team through RAA, PAA, TET, which will become an integral part of your team's performance to complete the Norming and Performing team dynamic process. Building your team through RAA, PAA, TET will provide the important fundamental elements to your team process or playbook for your team to follow along with setting up the right environment and culture for your team to succeed in. In the end you will be building your team through RAA, PAA, TET. Bringing it all together for your team through the team dynamics process, making it easy to follow, initiate, implement, incorporate, integrate and inspire within your team and always looking for areas of improvement along the way.

Process Dynamics

Process Dynamics	• The Essential Elements of Information (EEI) of Who, What, Where, When, How and Why
Process Mapping and Process Narrative	• Avoid the "5 Monkeys" • Team Mission Statement • Team Charter • Overall Team Process, Process Map and Workflow

A man places 5 monkeys in a room. Later in the day, he brings in a ladder, ties a banana from the ceiling near the top of the ladder and leaves the room. With the banana "just" hanging there, a monkey tries to climb the ladder to get to the banana. As soon as the monkey starts to climb the ladder, he and his buddies are sprayed with a water hose knocking him off the ladder and getting the others all wet. Another monkey decides to climb the ladder to get to the banana and faces the same bad result of getting sprayed and knocked off the ladder. This process continues with all 5 monkeys until they will not try climbing the ladder for fear of getting sprayed from the water hose.

The man removes a monkey from the room and replaces it with a new monkey. The new monkey sees the banana and decides to climb the ladder to get to the banana. As soon has he touches the ladder, the other 4 monkeys grab him, beat him and keep him from climbing the ladder out of fear of getting sprayed. This continues until the new monkey stops trying to climb the ladder out of the fear of getting held back and beaten by the other monkeys.

A second original monkey is removed from the room and replaced with a new monkey. As you can figure out, the new monkey tries to climb the ladder and gets the same bad result of getting held back and beaten by the other monkeys. This process continues until the last original monkey is removed from the room and replaced by the last new monkey. Once again, the last new monkey is held back, beaten and not allowed to get to the banana.

The other 4 new monkeys don't know why they keep the last new monkey from getting to the banana except for the fact that "We have always done it this way", even though it does nothing but produce negative results and no one really knows why the process is followed in the first place. Charles Kettering said: "If you have always done it that way, it is probably wrong." G.K Chesterton said: "It is not that they cannot see the solution. It is that they cannot see the problem." The problem as detailed with the 5 monkeys is an ineffective team process or culture that provides no value to the team. Don't let "We have always done it this way" become the culture for your team. The "We have always done it this way" creates a culture of "Yes Men", a bunch of puppets for your team where your team members do not have the ability to think on their own and cannot become independent, imaginative, creative and critical thinkers, an integral part of a successful team. A "We have always done it this way" along with an undocumented, poorly documented or sparsely documented team process or culture will have negative consequences if kept unchecked. A poorly documented team process or culture can lead to:

- Inconsistency, ambiguity and uncertainty amongst your team and any internal or external partners you may have.
- A lack in confidence in your team's ability to deliver.
- A badly beaten and bruised team.

When it comes to team culture, Edgar Schein said: "The bottom line for leaders is that if they do not become conscious of the cultures in which they are embedded, those cultures will manage them. Cultural understanding is desirable for all of us, but it is essential to leaders if they are to lead." One final thing on team culture. Setting up the right team culture starts at the top levels of your team for it to be fully effective.

Business Process Mapping and building your team – A Business Application

So now you know not to act like a bunch of monkeys, consider how a well-documented team process can bring value to your team. But before you do that, consider some of the rapid changes that are taking place in the work place today. No longer is your team tied to a desk to do their work. We have become a mobile workforce and through this change there is a lot of good that is taking place. New business processes on how to manage your team are continually popping up.

Today, a lot business process-oriented people are looking at more dynamic work place processes as being the way to address the changes which are taking place. Some of these people even feel that some team processes can become too structured and do not fully support the rapid changes we are experiencing today, but there is one common denominator in their processes as compared to what this book introduces. The one common denominator is that every team member needs to know and understand what their roles and responsibilities are in today's work place. The processes introduced in this book are no different than some of the new processes that are being introduced today. The team processes need to be very dynamic in nature, living documents where process changes are not frowned upon but encouraged when process improvements need to be made. By making your team process a dynamic living document open to change helps build a team of independent, imaginative, creative and critical thinkers, the key elements to a successful team. By making your team process a dynamic living document introduces an "entrepreneurial spiritual element" to your team process which helps your team when dealing with all the different types of scenarios or situations they may face. Building your team through RAA, PAA, TET helps you define your dynamic team process, and the team roles and responsibilities for handling the rapid changes that are taking place today.

The start of your Team Process

Your team process documentation begins after you have gathered your process building team through team dynamics. Your team process:

- Provides you the foundation that your team will work from.
- Represents your team philosophy and your team fundamentals.
- Represents your overall team playbook, the plays from which your team will follow.
- Is a process where individual and team creativity is encouraged from the members of your team.

And every time your team follows your team process, the "process steps" they are following and performing are "repeatable" and open to change, when change is required.

Essential Elements of Information, EEI

Through EEI, a well-documented team process will let your team know the Who, What, Where, When, How and Why within your process.

Utilizing EEI for generating the type of questions you will want to ask when defining your team process is essential. When defining your process, do so with a level of clarity where almost anyone could pick up the process and with little or no guidance be able to perform without failure. Stay focused on what you want to accomplish, a well-defined team process. EEI can provide you the proper level of clarity and focus that you need to have when defining your process. In addition to EEI, when trying to get to the level of clarity you need within your process, a series of "Why" questions or "The 5 Whys" type of question and answer session can also be extremely beneficial to help keep your eye on the target, focused on reaching your goal and delivering a well-defined and elaborate team process. Drill down up to 5 levels and use EEI to get to the level of clarity and focus you need when defining and elaborating on your process. When mapping out your team process using EEI, it is important to understand how people (human factors) and your business or operating support systems (B / OSS) interact, the "man and machines" of your operations.

It is also important to understand how your people and the business systems relate to your operations, your day-to-day activities directly and indirectly. Direct lines to and within your team process represent:

- What you are looking to accomplish, your team's key job functions and tasks and are integral to delivering a quality product to your customer.
- The process areas which your team owns and are part of your team's core competencies.
- And bring the greatest value to your team and have the greatest impacts within your team process which can positively or negatively affect your customer.

Indirect lines within your team process cover the ancillary areas that support your team. They are areas you typically don't own as a team and represent the support groups to your process. Indirect lines may belong to another institution's team, it could be from an internal or external partner or a third-party provider providing valuable support to your team. While they may seem less important when it comes to your process, they can be equally important when it comes to the quality of your product or project delivery, your budget or your schedule. Make sure you manage the working relationship you have with your internal and external partners when understanding the level of importance indirect lines may bring to you, your team or your customer.

Team Meetings

When documenting your team process, there will be a need for a series of informal and formal meetings to map out the process. These meetings will require the cooperation and collaboration from all that have an interest in your team process. Informal meetings can be as simple as a few team members coming together to discuss a plan of action related to a customer deliverable or to respond to a problem. Formal meetings can be complex involving multiple stakeholders related to, but not limited to:

- Customer requirements and deliverables.
- Progress and status updates.
- Strategic and / or tactical planning sessions.

When planning for all your team meetings, formal or informal, treat the preparation for them the same. Make sure your team members come to these meetings prepared. Proper preparation shows that you respect everyone's time and that you understand that time is the only non-renewable resource we have when it comes to these team meetings. Have the meeting agenda listed. Provide the guidelines or the rules of engagement for the meeting discussions and allocate the proper amount of time needed to accomplish your goals and objectives for the meeting and in the end ALWAYS promptly send out meeting minutes looking for feedback from your audience. Along with your meeting agenda there also will be a list of meeting objectives to work from. If you meet these objectives, then your meeting was a success. If you do not meet these objectives, then action items will come out of the meeting which must be assigned and addressed. When defining your list of meeting objectives, again be SMART in your approach, use EEI and "The 5 Whys" type of question and answer session along with the fundamental principles of building your team through RAA, PAA, TET. Make sure all action items are assigned to someone in the meeting that has the ability to address the action item and ensure that they are able to provide an update to the action item at your next meeting working towards closure of the action item.

When you set up your team meetings with your team stakeholders you will allocate as much time as needed to meet your meeting objectives. Should your team meeting require outside stakeholders, a good practice is to keep your meetings to no more an hour in length as this timeframe has been shown to be a productive use of everyone's time that are involved in the meeting. Based on this, there may be a series of meetings needed to accomplish your overall objective. There are a few reasons for keeping your meetings to no more than an hour in length.

- Most people lose interest in a prolonged discussion at around 45-minutes. As an example, take a look at TV programming or live stage performances. For most 1-hour TV programs, the actual program is only about 45-minutes long with commercial breaks dispersed throughout the program. Some live stage performances will perform for 45-minutes, have a brief intermission and finish up the play with another 45-minute performance. If your meeting does not have a "captive audience through stimulating conversation", then your audience will begin to lose interest at around the 45-minute mark.
- Everyone's time is valuable. By limiting your meetings, especially with your external stakeholders to no more than an hour in length, you are showing that you respect their time.
- If there is a need to go over an hour for your meetings, limit the number of times you meet in a given month for these long meetings, no more than twice a month.
- If there is a need for a marathon meeting (longer than a few hours), look to schedule them no more than once a month or once a quarter.

To make the meeting productive, send out your full meeting agenda prior to the meeting date with enough time for everyone to review the agenda and come prepared to the meeting. After you send out your agenda, if you feel that the agenda or meeting objectives are complex, reach out and touch base with your key meeting attendees to see if they have any questions that you can address prior to the meeting taking place.

When your team does meet, allow time towards the end of your meeting to have an open forum discussion. This will allow your team to discuss anything they deem important that is related to your project or product that may not have been part of the original meeting agenda. This also allows for flexibility within your meeting and the agenda you have planned and will bring added value to your meeting discussion.

Make sure the meeting minutes are provided to all stakeholders after your meeting is over that have an interest in your team process and make sure all action items are clearly defined and assigned within your meeting minutes with due dates for when the action items will be addressed and closed. Don't wait to send out your meeting minutes. Make time in your own schedule to getting the meeting minutes to all of your stakeholders in a timely manner. If you are allowed, you can record your meeting in place of sending out the meeting minutes. Just make sure you gain everyone's approval first and that everyone is in agreement of using the recordings in place of the meeting minutes.

Business Process Management (BPM) – A Business Application

Back in the 1990's to early 2000's, Business Process Management (BPM) became popular through its introduction of process modelling applications. BPM was one of the first automated tools when it came time to map out an organizations (team) workflow or team process, especially when it became time to define project or process requirements. Via BPM, one key goal is to externalize processes using an inside-out approach, "From within an organization to across organizations."

Another key requirement of BPM is the ability to collaborate with other business functions within and across the organization or institution. BPM has always been considered a way for bringing data, people and systems together. It was through BPM where it became important to note that business processes are collaborative. They involve people. If you decide to follow the BPM process, there are six functional elements within their framework to think about. You will:

- Define the overall team process via a process map (visual or graphical representation) and process narrative (written representation).
- Run and execute the team process which you have defined to identify any GAPs within your process.
- Manage the team process via value-added key performance indicators (KPIs).
- Integrate all people, external processes and applications to your team process.
- Connect all users to your team process. This will include suppliers (external partners), internal teams and customers.
- Reference and follow industry frameworks.

Moving forward in time and with the introduction of cloud technology, one of the key topics within the cloud framework is workflow process development. Technology and the "wording" of the process may change, but the fundamental framework, like business process management vs. workflow process management, behind the technology pretty much stays the same.

Industry Frameworks – A Business Application

One of these industry frameworks when it comes to workflow process development which you can consider is from SEI's CMMI for Services Model. SEI defines 24 CMMI for Services Process Areas which are broken out into categories or functional areas. These process areas are implemented at the different CMMI Capability and Maturity Levels which are tied back to Generic Goals and Practices within the CMMI. The 24 CMMI for Services Process Areas are:

- Service Establishment and Delivery.
    - Incident Resolution and Prevention.
    - Service Delivery.
    - Service System Development.
    - Service System Transition.
    - Strategic Service Management.
- Project Management.
    - Capacity and Availability Management.
    - Integrated Project Management.
    - Project Monitoring and Control.

- Project Planning.
- Quantitative Project Management.
- Requirements Management.
- Risk Management.
- Supplier Agreement Management.
- Service Continuity.
* Process Management.
  - Organizational Innovation and Deployment.
  - Organizational Process Definition.
  - Organizational Process Performance.
  - Organizational Training.
* Support.
  - Casual Analysis and Resolution.
  - Configuration Management.
  - Decision Analysis and Resolution.
  - Measurement and Analysis.
  - Process and Product Quality Assurance.

As each capability level or maturity level increases, the number of process areas used increases along with their complexity. Below are the different CMMI Generic Goals and Practices, Capability and Maturity Levels you can achieve within the CMMI for Services Process Areas.

Generic Goals and Practices	CMMI Capability Levels	CMMI Maturity Levels
Generic Goal 1 (GG 1)	1. Performed	1. NA
Generic Goal 2 (GG 2)	2. Managed	2. Managed
Generic Goal 3 (GG 3)	3. Defined	3. Defined
Generic Goal 4 (GG 4)	4. Quantitatively Managed	4. Quantitatively Managed
Generic Goal 5 (GG 5)	5. Optimizing	5. Optimizing

In addition to websites like SEI, there are also industry specific websites which define and support how their industry functions. As an example, for the telecommunications industry there is an organization called ATIS (Alliance for Telecommunication Industry Solutions; atis.org). ATIS provides the framework for how the carriers are to work together using a common framework that is set-up in scenario-based forums. One of these ATIS forums is the OBF for their Order and Billing Forum. In this forum, there are instructions for handling fulfillment orders and billing to customers covering every scenario imaginable. Feel free to visiting SEI's website (sei.cmu.edu/cmmi/) to learn more about their process areas and the different CMMI Capability and Maturity Levels along with the industry forum websites for their industry specific forums.

Team Mission Statement

When you begin mapping out your overall team process, include a team mission statement and team charter. The team mission statement and team charter are the starting points and high-level details of your team process. Your mission statement is the first place you should direct people to that has an interest in your team. Keep your mission statement simple and to the point. Your mission statement provides a brief summary of what your team does; your team's primary objectives and responsibilities. It defines your overall team goal. Make sure everyone on your team knows and understands your team mission statement.

Team Charter

The team mission statement should be a standalone document, but it can also be rolled into the team charter as an introductory piece of the charter should you wish to combine the two. Additional team details will be included in the team charter for your team to follow. It is the second-level of your overall team process documentation. Your team charter:

- Will begin with a title and executive summary.
- Is followed by a description of what your team represents along with the "business need or case" for why your team exists.
- Will identify the upper tier of your team's management team. You can also provide the authority levels the management team members have when it comes to them making decisions as they relate to leading your team.
- Where needed, will define your team resources as they relate to your product or project deliverables.

Responsibility, Accountability, Consulting, Informing (RACI) Model – A Business Application

When defining your team resources and what they do, this can include a Responsibility, Accountability, Consulting and Informing (RACI) Model which is used for empowering your team. The RACI Model, as shown in the table below, is a snapshot and cross-reference matrix of what you want to empower your team to do as it relates to your team process or your product delivery. A more detailed example of the RACI Model can be found in Appendix A.

Activity	Name 1	Name 2	Name 3
Analysis	R	R	I
Requirements	R, A	C	I
Design	A	R	C
Construction	A	R	C

You will identify your key team members or stakeholders within your RACI Model. This can also include external partners within your institution, your suppliers and your customers.

Now back to the team charter. You will define the key deliverables you have within your team along with the deliverables from your external partners as they relate to your customer. You can provide a constraints and assumptions section to your team charter if you want.

- A constraint is any limiting factor that can have an impact to a key deliverable.
- An assumption is something taken to be true, but may not be true as it pertains to a team function. Once an assumption is validated or found to be true it can become a business rule within your team charter. If the assumption is found to be untrue or false, it is simply removed from your team process.

Overall Team Process

The final part of your process documentation is your overall team process. Your team process is the final level in your process hierarchy. Your overall team process:

- Provides the guidelines on how your team is to perform and should cover every possible scenario your team can and will experience.
- Helps to ensure that the work your team performs is consistently followed leading to team performance effectiveness and efficiency.

- Follows after your team mission statement and team charter are complete.

In your team process, you will:

- Provide complete details for your team to include your process map. A process narrative supporting the process map can also be provided which are considered sub-sets to the overall team process.
- Cover the value-added steps that allows your team to be successful. Process steps that provide no value to your team or to your customer should not be part of your team process.
- Provide the functional layers within your team and it is up to you to peel back these layers for your team to be successful.

A prime example of peeling back the layers is the process of kicking a field goal in a football game. When the placekicker kicks the football, it is important for the placeholder to make sure the football laces are pointing away from the placekicker's foot and the placeholder is not just placing the football on the ground for the placekicker to kick. This key process step prevents any unnecessary spin to the football when the placekicker kicks the football caused by the football laces coming into contact with the placekicker's foot. By peeling back the layers, you will instill even greater confidence into the team by showing them that attention to details are extremely important when it comes to your team process. It shows that attention to details are critical when leading a team and that all good leaders and their team members possess this trait.

Another great example of the importance a team process can bring to you and your team comes from the article *Eye to Eye with Ebola, Lessons in safety and unity in treating 4 US patients* from the ENA Connection magazine by Amy Carpenter Aquino. In Amy's article, one of the Chief Clinical Nurses at the Emory University Hospital in Atlanta, GA addressed how her team would treat the Ebola virus once it came to the US. The Chief Clinical Nurse and her team created a team process to address the threat of the Ebola virus in the US. The Chief Nurse said: "Keeping the staff, patients and community safe was their number 1 priority by setting up a foundation, a culture of safety and accountability through their SOP. Consistency was really important in how we did things. Ensuring that all involved followed the SOP, which is where accountability came into play." Your overall team process, like an SOP represents your team fundamentals along with the plays within your playbook covering every scenario and as the nursing team experienced it can come down to life or death situations.

Process Map and Narrative as part of your overall Team Process

As stated before, your process narrative in support of your process map is a sub-set of your overall written team process and represents the written version of your process map. The process map is a visual or graphical representation of your process and is also considered a sub-set of your overall team process. Your process map can be created in two forms:

- Transactional where the process is mapped out beginning-to-end where each of your team names is assigned to the process step.
- Cross-functional (swim lanes) mapped out beginning-to-end crossing the team name boundaries as the process progresses.

Appendix A provides examples of the 2 types of process maps defined above. Your process map will have process steps, decision points and process annotations to show the flow-of-work your team will perform. In the telecommunications field, the acronyms MACD (Move, Add, Change and Disconnect or Delete) and New are used to help make sure every scenario is covered (as a reference, MACD - New is also covered in the industry forum website for ATIS). When defining your overall team process, make sure you cover every possible scenario-type your team will experience. Define the scenarios which:

- Are considered in-scope to your team and your customer deliverables.
- Meet your expectations and bring value to your team when it comes to your customer's expectations.

Also include a section in your team process defining the out-of-scope scenarios which your team is not responsible for or are not part of a customer deliverable.

Reviewing the team process with your team is part of your team's on-boarding or indoctrination process. Based on this, have an on-boarding process in place for when new team members join your team. This makes their integration into your team occur so much easier than just throwing them into the deep end to see if they will sink or swim. The team process provides the full details for your team to follow and represents the "core elements" of your team's responsibilities, your team's expectations.

You will need to remove the "What Ifs" in your team process documentation where you can by addressing them up front. It does not mean you ignore them completely as some can actually be beneficial to you as you look to make improvements based on some simple questions like: "What if we did it this way?" "Have we looked at this approach in our team process to make it better?" If there are improvements that can be made it does not hurt to look into them knowing how they relate to your team process improvement initiatives.

One final note on your team process as it pertains to this book. Throughout the book, we will reference your team process, the team playbook and sometimes the SOP. Within the confines of this book, your team process, the team playbook and a SOP are synonymous of one another, each representing the same thing.

Active Listening

Being an active listener is important when you start your team process mapping exercise. A good leader has the ability to listen to their team members. They are active listeners where they learn to listen and listen to learn. Stephen Covey said: "Listening involves patience, openness, and the desire to understand – highly developed qualities of character." Dr. Robert J. Bies said: "You want to create opportunities for "Voice" and "Listen." Allow people to voice their ideas and opinions; listen to them; and be disciplined and patient when they are doing so. Listening is one of the most important leadership principles you should learn. Through your active listening you make people feel valuable and a part of your team.

Once you have mastered the art of active listening, then you will have the ability to pass on this wonderful trait to all your team members. All inputs from your team and any feedback you get from anyone else (an outside stakeholder) that has an interest in your team process should be considered valuable. This sets up an open agenda which you will work from. You should listen to what all your team stakeholders have to say.

Don't just disregard their inputs and feedback without first discussing them with your team and knowing what their impacts may be when it comes to your team process. Ken Blanchard and Spencer Johnson said: "Feedback is the breakfast of champions." "Feed on it" to get the results you want. Because you as a leader are an active listener when it comes to your team process provides proof to everyone that you look to your team process as being a living document. One that is open to change. When team process change is required, make the change. Communicate to everyone that has an interest in your team process that you are making the change and gain their buy-in. This will keep them up-to-date and keeps you away from "unexpected results" by maintaining an open communication channel. This also shows to your team, your internal and external partners and even your customers that you are adaptable to change, which in today's business world can be extremely vital to any team process.

Be SMART

When you start mapping out your team process, be SMART in your approach. Use the SMART acronym. Not only is it important and useful in project management, it is very important and useful when you start defining the "realistic" requirements for your team process. When it comes to SMART:

- Be Specific when defining your team process steps ensuring they are Measurable.
- Create value-added key performance indicators (KPIs) to help measure your team process effectiveness.
- Understand the "takt time" and how long it takes to complete each process step and the overall process life cycle itself (Note: In Lean Six Sigma, takt time is the rate at which a finished product needs to be completed in order to meet customer demand). Removing all non-value-added elements in your team process will improve your takt time and it allows you to meet your deliverables to your customer on-time and in most cases, under budget.
- Provide customer SLAs or Service Level Agreements, where they are needed and always look for improvements to your SLAs where they exist.
- Make sure all customer deliverables that come out of your team process are Achievable, Attainable and Realistic.

- Allow your team the time to achieve the results you want and what your customer expects.
- Make sure all team process requirements are attainable and realistic when defining your team process.
- Remove all excessive non-productive elements from your team process (too many non-productive e-mails, too many non-productive meetings, as an example).

Peter Drucker said: "Meetings are by definition a concession to a deficient organization. For one either meets or one works. One cannot do both at the same time." If you don't give your team members enough time to complete their work, how can you expect them to deliver a quality product? They will become "burned out" putting in the overtime to meet your customer deliverable if they not given the time to deliver a quality product when they are tied up in long non-productive meetings.

Shane Parrish of Farnam Street not long ago wrote an excellent article about Warren Buffet entitled, *What Warren Buffet would say about your stressful work environment*. In the article Shane talked about distractions that can occur in large organizations. How Warren Buffet deals with it, he removes the distractions from his workplace to allow himself time to read, think and do things he sees as being important. The key point from the article is to set-up your team environment to allow your team to perform their job when it comes to your customers. Remove the excessive, non-productive elements from your team process. As Shane states in his article, "Environments play an important role on individual and collective abilities to make decisions and yet, most organizations spend zero time thinking about this." Now back to SMART:

- Make sure you manage all your team meetings effectively to set-up your team environment for your team's success. A well-documented team process helps eliminate non-productive excessive meetings that cost valuable production time.
- Negotiate with your customer the "achievable" delivery timelines and make sure you can meet them, but under no circumstance try to meet an unrealistic deliverable because that is "What management or the customer expects." Unrealistic management or customer expectations can lead to re-work and additional costs.
- Stay within the confines of your realistic requirements and timelines, which leads us to the final piece to your "SMART" team process

which is Timeliness. Now that you have negotiated an acceptable delivery time with your customer, make sure you can meet the timeline with a quality product.

Now that you have started mapping out your team process, make sure your team is aware of its importance for delivering a quality product to your customer and look for input from them. Having your team members or even your customer, where you are allowed, involved in the team process creation creates a collaborative work environment for your team and your customer. A team process mapped in a vacuum or a silo, stays in the vacuum or the silo, never leaves the vacuum or the silo and no one will use it, let alone fully understand it. A good collaborative team process is a living document open to change and provides your team the meaningful direction they will follow and work against. It sets up an overall open agenda for your team to follow.

Self-Interests and Hidden Agendas

You should always stay away from "self-interests and hidden agendas" within your team process. This is not the agendas for meetings but the hidden agendas some people and "bosses" bring with them like, "I am going to get this promotion and I don't care who I have to step on or over to get it." President Theodore Roosevelt stated it best: "People ask the difference between a leader and a boss. The leader leads, and the boss drives."

- These "so-called Bosses" will override the team process by exercising poor judgement with the intent of their own personal gain.
- Bosses driven by self-interests are not leaders nor are they team players. Some of them are "Yes Men", or Puppets driven by a Puppet Master.
- The "Boss" or the "Yes Men" show no loyalty towards the team. They only care about themselves and bring no value to a successful team environment.
- They kill the "teamwork" effort and damage your team.

These self-interests and hidden agendas can be your own (if you feel "Bossy") or even placed upon you by your "Bossy" superiors as they look to advance in the institution at the expense of using you. Avoid them as much as possible. Self-interests and hidden agendas:

- Lead to inconsistency, ambiguity and team uncertainty, because in most cases, their hidden agendas are never well communicated to the team.
- Misdirect your team from the ultimate goal which is delivering a quality product to your customer.

With self-interests or hidden agendas, how can you ever expect your team to trust your decisions let alone trust you? How can you expect your team to respect you if they don't trust you? How can you expect full active participation from your team members if there are self-interests or hidden agendas?

An Open Agenda

By working with an open agenda that everyone is on-board and actively participating in, you will have the potential for unlimited success. And when it comes to active participation, Jack Welch said: "It is a culture that breeds an endless search for ideas that stand or fall on their merits, rather than the rank of their originator, a culture that brings every mind into the game." Through this everyone needs to participate bringing their intellectual capital to the game for your team's success.

Jeffrey Gitomer said: "Respect and credibility lead to trust with your customer." Warren Buffet said: "Trust is like the air we breathe. When it's present, nobody really notices, but when it is absent, everybody notices." This also applies to your team if you expect them to fully trust and respect you. Your open agenda will help provide the level of trust and respect you need to effectively lead your team.

A good example for respect comes from the movie, *Master and Commander, The Far Side of the World*. In the movie, Captain "Lucky" Jack Aubrey explains to a young Midshipman that "True leadership and the right to earn your crew's respect comes from strength and discipline." It takes the right combination of strength and discipline to earn your team's respect, to be a true leader. Another good example for respect comes from the movie, *The Replacements*. In the movie, Coach McGinty runs into Shane Falco the night before their first game, both of them nervous about the upcoming game. In their discussion, Coach McGinty tells Shane to: "Find a way to lead your team, earn their respect." Building your team through RAA, PAA, TET will provide you the principles needed for leading your team where you can earn their trust and respect. Remember, "Respect is earned and not given." Also remember this which they state in the movie, *TAPS*, "The loyalty of men is always hard earned." This is especially true when it comes to earning the trust, respect and loyalty of your team and others around you.

Buy-in and Sign-off

Once you have your team mission statement, the team charter and overall team process complete, the final piece to your process is to get buy-in and sign-off for your process from everyone involved in its creation. Your external partners and your customers can also provide approval and buy-in, where needed. It has also been said that "People are going to buy-in what they can put their hands on." Get your team process out in front of all the interested parties and let them put their hands on your process so that you can get their buy-in and sign-off. Now that your team process is complete and you have received buy-in from everyone, let the rest of your institution know that you are "open for business" with a detailed team process that works. Let the other institutional teams know that you are always open to listening to their feedback and for areas of improvement when it comes to your open agenda and your team process.

Communication

"Communication is the secret to success. Pass it on." When it comes to defining and explaining your team process or even the deliverables to your customer, COMMUNICATE! You will communicate early and often within your team and to your customer. Don't wait until there is a formal team meeting to communicate important items or deliverables to your team or to your customer.

Make readily available your contact information and your team's contact information to all that have an interest in it, especially when it comes to your customer deliverables. This way, should someone need to contact you or your team they will be able to find the contact information very easily. Include ALL your contact information in your voicemails, e-mails and all other forms of communication, formal and informal to your suppliers (external partners), internal teams and your customers.

Even the best documented team process brings no value if it is not properly communicated to all who will use it or benefit from it. This includes all customers, internal / external partners, direct or indirect. Always maintain open communication with your partners and your customers. Make sure your customers, internal and external, know your team process, where you are allowed and what the benefits are for having a well-documented process in place. Provide the tools and the structure for good communication and let your customer know that their input will be well received and feedback will be provided to their inquiries.

Don't be afraid of communicating the bad along with the good when it comes to your team process or your customer. A lot of times people are afraid to communicate the bad because it shows a weakness in their process. You cannot improve unless you communicate the bad along with the good. When we don't communicate the bad, we leave something out in our communication. This can lead to your team or your customer asking all kinds of questions, sounding like a bunch of little kids on a very long trip, "Are we there yet, are we there yet?" "Where are we at?" "When can we expect to get there?" "Are we there yet?" Pretty annoying isn't it. Effective and open communication eliminates the need for excessive questions like "Are we there yet?" It builds trust between you, your team and your customer.

Should your team process change, understand the impacts the changes will have on your customer and document and communicate the change to all of your direct and indirect lines and once again look for their feedback and buy-in.

Team Process Repository or Library

Now that your team process is complete, set up a process repository, a process library for storing your process. Look to providing a repository structure that is consistent across your institution that everyone can agree upon. Build a common naming structure and hierarchy for your process repository or library across your entire institution and tell everyone where and how they can find your team process when they need to find it. This way when other teams within your institution begin documenting their own team processes, the institutional team processes can be easily found without someone having to ask for them or having to ask where the latest version can be found. Don't just communicate that the institutional team processes are "On SharePoint or on the shared drive" if you don't have a common institutional-defined process repository or library in place.

Telling someone that your team process is "On SharePoint or on the shared drive" without direction or having a common repository or library in place is like telling someone your car is in the parking lot at a sold-out Ohio State University Buckeyes football game. GOOD LUCK in finding that without direction or a little help!

For your external partners and customers, where you are allowed, you can place your institutional team process documents on your web-page and allow your external partners or your customers access to the web-page and your institutional team processes.

We have covered a lot of information, right? Now it is time to get into the main purpose of this book. We have defined our approach, now we are ready to get into the "meat" of this book, RAA, PAA, TET; The Power to Motivate People. Building your team through RAA, PAA, TET. The Playbook for Success. ENJOY!

The Contract

| The Contract | • Your Contract and your Team Member's Contract |

Before you start the process of building your team through RAA, PAA, TET, you can have a contract or a letter of intent between yourself and your team members. In the movie, *Coach Carter*, the Coach and his student-athletes signed a contract that set the expectations for the team. Everyone on the team, including Coach Carter, had to live up to these expectations if they wanted to be part of the team. The team member signatures showed that they were committed to live up to the high standards set in the contract. For your team following Coach Carter's example, you can initiate a contract which you will provide to each team member. This team member contract can:

- Be a single page contract to a multiple page contract based on your expectations for your team members.
- Provide the high-level details and expectations which each team member is empowered and entrusted to perform.
- Include the high-level individual responsibilities, accountabilities and levels of authority for each team member as it relates to your team process.
- Include the high-level items that they are expected to achieve and the relationships they will need to build and maintain to be a part of an effective team.
- Provide the high-level details for the lesson plan used in teaching the team members the fundamental principles and techniques needed to be successful.

This contract and the lesson plans will be living documents and can be modified based on the individual team member's performance, especially in areas of improvement for the team member.

This contract will be tied back to:

- The vision, to the strategic and tactical plans that you have set for your team.
- Your team process.
- Your team's primary and secondary job guidelines which are defined in the next section of this book.
- Your lesson plans for the mentoring of your team members and for any individual and / or team process improvement initiatives you may take.

Power – Responsibility, Accountability, Authority

Building your team	• Power, Motivation and People along with taking the initiative
• Power	• Responsibility – Defined Roles and Responsibilities, RACI Model and Job Guidelines with meaning and direction • Accountability – Defined Areas of Accountability, Ownership and Decision Making • Authority – Defined Authority Levels and Decision Making

Power - ability to act or produce an effect; possession of control, authority or influence over others.

Stephen Covey said: "Power is the faculty or capacity to act, the strength and potency to accomplish something." How we act and what we do, for the good or the bad, will determine how well you and your team will perform.

The Power focus in this book is about the team. Individual power from the 7 types of Power is summarized in the self-directed part of this section.

A great team reference comes from the famous baseball comic routine first done by Abbott and Costello in the late 1930's. In their comic routine all the baseball players have unique names like Who (1st base), What (2nd base), I Don't Know (3rd base), Why (LF) and Because (CF), just to name a few. The skit starts with Who's on 1st, What's on 2nd, I Don't Know is on 3rd. It is a brilliant comic routine from which Power and RAA, PAA, TET will provide you the answers to Who is on 1st, What is on 2nd and I Don't Know is on 3rd base. Power and RAA, PAA, TET will also keep you from screaming HEY ABBOTT!!!!, as Costello would do when things got a little hectic for the comedy team.

Effective Leadership

Power is a foundational building block for effective leadership. One of the best definitions of being an effective leader is someone that has the ability to influence others into doing something they normally would not do on their own. Properly influencing the institution is the ability to get things done, to work towards a common goal. Stephen Covey said: "Effective leadership is the only competitive advantage that will endure. That's because leadership has two sides – what a person is, his character, and what a person does, his competency." When it comes to one's character, Stephen went on to say: "What we *are* communicates far more eloquently than anything we *say or do*. We all know it. There are people we trust absolutely because we know their character." As a leader, you lead by example. As a leader, you set the example. These are key leadership traits which are taught in the US Army to help you in leading your team along with you earning your team's respect and trust. Mutual respect and trust are key to effective leadership.

From the AMC television show, <u>Mad Men and the episode Waterloo</u>, Bert tells Roger that "A leader is loyal to his team." It is up to you as a leader to be loyal to your team through the example you set. As a leader, you set the expectations for your team to follow that can influence your team at getting things done on time and done right. Peter Drucker and Warren Bennis both said: "Management is doing things right. Leadership is doing the right things." From the movie, <u>Remember the Titans,</u> one of the top football players told another top football player that "Attitude reflects leadership." It is up to you as a leader to do the right things and to have the right attitude towards your team when you do so. It is up to you as a leader to pass along the right attitude to your team when it comes to setting their targets, the expectations and the ground rules which they will play from as written in YOUR PLAYBOOK.

Empowerment

Power is empowerment. You want to empower your people to think and act independently. It frees up your time and allows you to focus on the one thing a leader does: To LEAD! It allows you to focus on the TI VUM long range strategic planning and pushes the tactical responsibilities down to your team. When your team walks out onto the playing field or court, you want to empower them for executing the plays in your playbook. Remember, your team process is your playbook. You want:

- Your team to hit the targets that have been set for them in your playbook.
- To ensure these targets are realistic and attainable, but not too low where anyone can reach them.
- To fully document through your playbook, what you are empowering your team to do and make sure they fully understand what their job is as it relates to your playbook. So many times, a team leader will look towards empowering their people, but will not provide the meaningful direction through a well-thought out team playbook.
- Your team to take charge and be in control of the tactical responsibilities that comes with being part of your team.

Empowerment will make them feel that they are an integral part of the team and gives them the controls to take charge. Empowerment shows them that you trust them in the decision-making process for the areas they are responsible and accountable for and gives them the authority to make decisions important to your team and to your customer. It sets up the right environment for your team.

Persuasion over Use of Force

When it comes to persuasion, an Aesop's fable of the Sun and the Wind is a perfect example. The Sun and Wind are arguing about who is more powerful until they see a traveler on the road below. They agree that the winner of the argument would be the first one that could remove the traveler's cloak from him. The Wind goes first and blows repeatedly as hard as he can trying to remove the cloak from the traveler only to have the traveler pull his cloak tighter to his body each time the Wind blows until the Wind decides to give up.

Now it is the Sun's turn. The Sun does what the Sun does best and shines bright and hot down on the traveler warming him until the traveler decides to take off his cloak because of the warmth provided by the Sun. The moral of the story is that: "Through persuasion your people will do things for you that force cannot compel them to do." President Abraham Lincoln, from his Temperance speech of 1842 said this of persuasion:

"When the conduct of men is designed to be influenced, persuasion, *kind, unassuming persuasion,* should ever be adopted."

Micro-management

One final thing about empowerment, DO NOT micro-manage the people on your team through excessive meetings or excessive control. Micro-management defeats the purpose when it comes to empowering your team. One example of micro-managing is controlling your team's work schedule and what they do. If your team is meeting the goals set by you along with putting in the required hours for getting the work done along with satisfying the customer, then having them show up at a set time may be counter-productive to their customer deliverables. Productive time is value added time and your team member that has the direct working relationship with your customer will understand your customer needs better than anyone on the outside looking in. Besides, being flexible in the work schedule and when the team member shows up to work creates the work-life balance every team member looks to achieve and no one is better at knowing the work-life balance than the individual team member, especially when it comes to their customers.

This leads us to our first building block; Power. Power is the first part of your foundation building blocks. This foundation contains three important parts – RAA. RAA stands for Responsibility, Accountability and Authority. There is a reason that Power and RAA is the first part of the foundation. RAA provides the:

- Fundamental direction as it pertains to your team's goals.
- Fundamental direction for your team to follow.
- Fundamental essentials to your team's success.

Responsibility - moral, legal or mental accountability; reliable; trustworthy.

Responsibility is directly related to the work that your team members perform. With responsibility your team members will have defined roles and responsibilities. They are entrusted to getting the work done.

Building Trust: The 4 C's

Before you can entrust your team, you will need to build up their trust through the 4 C's. Building trust includes the following:

- Character which includes integrity, honesty and respect for others.
- Competency which includes knowledge, skills and expertise along with having the ability to deliver reliable and responsive results.
- Consistency which includes WYSIWYD, What You Say is What You Do (ALWAYS lead by example). Deliver on promises and understand the power of explanation.
- Centricity where Other-Centric (I am thinking about you) overcomes Self-Centric (It's all about me).

Building trust from the 4 C's leads us to the items you can create when applying the RAA principles for power.

Responsibility, Accountability, Consulting, Informing (RACI) Model – A Business Application

One of the first key steps for this can be accomplished by creating a RACI Model for your team which defines what they are directly and indirectly responsible for within your team process or for your product or project delivery to your customer. A more detailed RACI Model example can be found in Appendix A of this book.

RACI Model Example

Activity	Name 1	Name 2	Name 3
Analysis	R	R	I
Requirements	R, A	C	I
Design	A	R	C
Construction	A	R	C

If you remember from the Process Dynamics section, the RACI Model is a matrix, a quick snapshot or cross-reference of what you want to empower your team to do as it relates to your overall team process or product. Items of direct responsibility represent your team's fundamental core competencies. They have the greatest impact to your customer. If your work is project-based, a RACI Model is considered one of your standard project management deliverables. It is one of your first key deliverables while you are in the project planning process. Your team also needs to know what they are indirectly responsible for. Items of indirect responsibility are for the support items you will deliver to your customer. Map out the direct and indirect responsibilities for your team as they fit within your overall team process. The RACI Model is:

- The first place where you create and build the identity of your team members. The type of team member you want them to be.
- Part of your team process, your playbook. Make sure you integrate the RACI Model into your team's playbook.

Job Guidelines – A Business Application

For your job guidelines to be effective, make sure they:

- Are tied back to your team playbook.
- Cover the fundamentals each of your team members are responsible for when it comes to your team and their playbook.

John C. Maxwell said: "One of the key hallmarks of successful leadership is knowing where every person adds value. Take some time to define each team member's area of contribution (including your own) and figure out how they all work together to make the team most effective." Jeff Haden for Inc.com wrote an article on Google's leadership. In the article, Jeff stated that: "Google's leadership team set up standards and guidelines that set up autonomy and independence for their team members, which gives them the responsibility and authority to do what is right, through the guidelines that have been set."

With these two quotes in mind, this is where job guidelines can come into play. Also, to help explain the importance job guidelines can play and your role when defining them, we will use a simple analogy for fielding a football team. When we look at the football team as a whole unit, you will have each player on the team fill a unique role or position like Cornerback, Linebacker, Offensive Line (Center), Tailback, etc. Each player on the team will then have fundamental direct and indirect responsibilities based on the position they play. They will also have Coaches that are experts in their field that teach them the fundamentals for the position they are assigned to play (DB Coach, LB Coach, O-Line Coach, RB Coach). The positional direct and indirect roles and responsibilities which each of these team players are taught to perform will:

- Be incorporated as part of the overall team playbook.
- As part of your team playbook, provide the key plays the team will execute as an integrated unit when they step out onto the field of play.

A great example of this when it comes to the position your team member's play comes from the 2013 Iron Bowl college football game between Auburn University and the University of Alabama. At the end of game time regulation, Alabama Head Coach Nick Saban decided to go for a long field goal try to win the game only to have the kick come up short and an Auburn Cornerback return the missed field goal for a game winning touchdown. All the conditions were right for Alabama.

- The field goal was within the range of the placekicker's ability.
- The wind was to the placekicker's back.
- There was only 1 second left on the clock.
- The chances for Auburn returning the football for a touchdown were extremely small.

Everything was near perfect until the miss and Alabama suddenly learned that they had 8 Offensive Linemen on the field that did not have the speed or the agility to chase down an elusive returning Auburn Cornerback. The makeup of your team is no different than that of fielding a football team and the primary position that each of your team members are taught and expected to play. Job guidelines:

- Help to define the complex critical job functions, the direct responsibilities for your team members.
- Represent the detailed primary functions (roles and responsibilities) each of your team members will perform within your team's playbook.
- Represents their core competencies.
- Provide "meaning and clear direction through meaningful work" for your team members. Job guidelines that have no meaning or clear direction can seem trivial or menial to the team member.

- Help complete the build of your team member's identities.
- Includes the feedback from your team members because there is no one better at defining their work than the actual person performing it. Walk through, observe and where you can, perform the job functions with your team members as you are defining their job guidelines because there no better way to understanding what your team does than by observing or performing the job first hand. You will earn your team's respect if you are willing to put your "Boots on the ground" observing or performing the jobs they perform.
- When defined, can include you engaging your customers to gain their feedback as their input can be extremely valuable when it comes to your customer deliverables.

And finally, when defining your team members job guidelines, it is your responsibility as a leader to define what your team fundamentally does and to make sure each team member understands the job you are entrusting them to do. Your team's job guidelines help you when it comes time for building your team's trust. As stated before and no different than the RACI Model, your job guidelines will need to be integrated within your team process.

For your RACI Model, job guidelines and the team process, you will provide the title for the role your team member will fill, like Quarterback, Half Back, Linebacker, Director, Team Lead, Project Manager or Analyst, to name a few. As you go back to the RACI Model.

- Your team's primary job functions are the ones they have direct responsibility for.
- These primary job functions have the greatest customer impacts and form a direct line to your customer needs.

Anthony Ulwick is the author of the book entitled _"What Customers Want"_. Not long ago, Anthony wrote an article for MarketingJournal.org entitled _Best Practice: Uncovering Unmet Customer Needs_. In the article, Anthony detailed a four-step approach for capturing the desired outcomes from your customer to meet your customer's needs. Within his four-step approach, the 1st step Anthony defined was called job mapping. As defined in the article:

- Job mapping is where you dissect the job the customer is trying to get done into process steps.
- This job mapping can provide you a clear understanding for the job your team member will perform from a customer's perspective.

In a lot of ways, this job mapping exercise is no different than the process mapping steps you would take when defining your team process. By breaking down the job into process steps can be very beneficial when:

- Defining the job guidelines your team member will perform to meet your customer's needs.
- It comes down to the team member's identity and the job boundaries that can exist when it comes to your team process.

Your job guidelines should define what is in-scope and out-of-scope for your team members when it comes to your customer deliverables. Your job guidelines can also define the secondary job functions for your team members. Secondary job functions have a more indirect line to your customer's needs and depending on the scenario, are less important than the direct line items when it comes to your customer deliverables. It is still important to know the secondary job function impacts and how they relate to your customer and what your team's responsibilities are for these secondary job functions. It is also important to differentiate between the primary job functions and the secondary job functions should you decide to include the secondary job functions in your job guidelines.

You should always look to the job guidelines as being used for important critical primary job functions, but what do you use for these less critical duties, the secondary job functions, should you decide to separate them from your team member's primary job guidelines? This is where you can use task lists, as an option for defining and listing your team's secondary job guidelines.

Task Lists Option – A Business Application

Task lists define and can be used for the less critical team roles, the indirect responsibilities and the secondary job functions which can be standalone from the primary job guidelines for the team members in these less critical roles. They will also need to be integrated into your team playbook should you decide to go the task list option route.

Task lists can also be used for communicating the frequency for when a job or a task is performed. This "frequency" for when a job function or a task is performed can also be included in your primary job guidelines for the direct responsibilities your team member will perform.

When you create your job guidelines and task lists, do so with enough clarity and focus that if someone new joins your team, they can follow the job guidelines and task lists and be able to perform the job or the task with little or no overview or supervision. Make sure they are easy to understand and that they are well understood by everyone on your team along with anyone outside your team that you support that has an interest in what your team does. Tie the job guidelines and task lists back to your:

- Team's playbook and the contract which has been set-up between yourself as a leader and your team members as they are inter-related.
- Customer deliverables and the targets which have been set for your team based on these deliverables.

If your team's jobs or tasks are not clearly defined.

- There can be and usually are delays in your customer deliverables.
- There can be inconsistency, ambiguity and uncertainty amongst your team.
- Failure to clearly define what your team does leads to "That's not my job" amongst your team members because of this uncertainty.
- Your team will hesitate or even second guess the quality of the product they need to deliver to your customer.
- Your team's confidence will diminish based on this uncertainty.

When it comes to creating your team's job guidelines and task lists be SMART in your approach, use EEI and "The 5 Whys" drill down type of question and answer session along with the principles of building your team through RAA, PAA, TET to help define what your team's jobs or tasks are. This can help remove any ambiguity and uncertainty when it comes to defining your team's responsibilities. It can help ensure that your team is confident in what their job is when it comes to your customer's deliverables. Using EEI as the basis, key questions for your job guidelines and task lists as they relate to your team process can include, but are not limited to:

- Who is responsible or accountable for a particular team process step, job function or task?
- Who is in your chain-of-command?
- Who are the decision makers?
- Who do they report to?
- Who reports to them?
- Who is their customer?
- What is their job title?
- What are their primary job functions and duties, their roles and responsibilities, directly related to your customer deliverables?
- What indirect responsibilities do they have?
- What kind of decisions can individual team members make?
- What level of decision making is allocated to the team members?
- What is the resource percent (%) allocated to a particular job function or task within a given work week or work reporting period?
- What are the status and reporting periods?
- What format is information stored in?
- What are the priority levels for your team?
- What are your key deliverables?
- What is in-scope (specified work that will be done) and out-of-scope (specifically identified work that will not be done) when it comes to customer deliverables?
- What are the team interdependencies when it comes to dealing with your customer?
- What are the team interdependencies within your own team or institution?
- What are your primary formal and informal forms of communication, internally and externally?
- Where does your team work? Is working remotely a possibility?
- Where is information stored?
- When are your status and progress reports due?
- When are your team deliverables due internally within your institution and externally to your external partners and / or to your customers?

- How much resource time is allocated to a particular job function or task within a given work week or work reporting period?
- How much authority is given to individual team members in the decision-making process?
- How is information stored?
- How do teams interact?
- How is information between teams disseminated and by what means?
- How are formal and informal communications handled?
- Why do your team members perform a particular job function or task?
- Why is it important and to whom is it important to?

You will notice, by using EEI there are some questions that are repeated. They are only asked differently, separating themselves from one another. That is the great thing about EEI. If done properly, every type of question or scenario will be asked and answered. Nothing will be left to chance. These are just a "few of the many" types of the questions you can ask when defining your team's responsibilities. With you knowing how your team operates, it's up to you to shorten the list or to come up with more.

Also, when it comes to defining your team's job guidelines and task lists, stay away from "Duties as Assigned", as being part of the primary job functions for your team. "Duties as Assigned" is setting your team up to being mostly reactive vs. being fully proactive when it comes to your team performing their jobs or their tasks. When a new job function or task is added to your team, make an update to the RACI Model, the job guidelines and / or the task lists for the new job function or task. Your RACI Model, job guidelines and task lists are:

- Living dynamic documents, no different than your team process when it comes to leading your team and dealing with change.
- Part of your team process on-boarding process for new team members joining the team. This will help remove any uncertainties a new team member may have when they first join your team.

Accountability - an obligation or willingness to accept responsibility

Accountability starts by defining and setting up the areas of accountability for your team members. Accountability when combined with responsibility equals ownership. Once you reach this level within your team, there is nothing your team cannot accomplish if they set their minds to it. Accountable job functions are the direct fundamental primary job functions within your team process. They have the greatest impact to your customer deliverables. Without accountability, customer deliverables will be missed and what is delivered will be a low-quality product that you will have to re-work if your customer does not dump you before you get to that point.

As said before, combining accountability with responsibility equals ownership. By combining accountability and responsibility, you are entrusting your team further within your team process. By pushing the levels of accountability down to your team, you are empowering them to be more successful. No longer will they feel like a number and more as an integral part of a successful team. Empowering your team will keep them actively engaged. Empowering your team shows that you trust them and that you know they are reliable for getting the job or the task done and done right. They are part of a team where there is active participation, they are fully engaged and with this in place they will be more enthusiastic in your team's success. Your open team agenda also helps keeping them fully engaged.

You will relate accountability to a team member's role. Role clarity is essential to your team's success when it comes to responsibility, accountability, authority and product or project job boundaries.

With Responsibility and Accountability (RA), you now have the first two parts of your RACI Model. Remember, the RACI Model provides your team a matrix summary of what they are doing. The RACI Model:

- Gives them the fundamental direction that they need.
- Addresses the areas they directly own.
- Helps to define the job boundaries that come with every job or task a person will look to fill within your team.

The last part of the RACI Model includes Consulting and Informing (CI). CI is where some of your indirect responsibilities or relations come into play with other institutional teams. There can also be some direct CI responsibilities and relationships to your team process. Where they exist, make sure they are also well defined and understood by your team.

Within the indirect responsibilities or relationships your team will have with other "outside" teams, it is important to hold these outside teams accountable for:

- The deliverables they will have with your customer. The deliverables they are responsible for delivering to your customer.
- Their results and their own decision-making process when it comes to your customer. Understand and know the impacts their team processes can have to your team process and your customer.

By understanding the direct and indirect relationships within your institution, you now are an integrated institution where silos are broken down and open communication channels exist.

Referring back to the article *Eye to Eye with Ebola, Lessons in safety and unity in treating 4 US patients*, the Chief Clinical Nurse said: "Accountability and following the SOP were always at the top of her teams list, their number 1 priority. Holding each other accountable and not being afraid to speak up is so powerful. That's really what kept us safe. Our lives depended on holding each other accountable; it depended on us doing the right thing every single time."

Now that your team is fully accountable, that accountability is part of your team culture through your team process, you will want to measure your team's success.

- Create checklists for your team's work to address accountability issues as they appear.
- Continually review your team's performance and provide timely feedback, good or bad, to your team as to their performance for delivering a quality product to your customer. When addressing individual work performance, do so in a closed setting maintaining the team member's privacy.
- Incorporate the Seven Tools of Quality Management along with the other quality management tools, which are defined towards the end of this book, into your team process when measuring your team's success.

Authority - power to influence or command thought, opinion or behavior; an individual cited or appealed to as an expert; persons in command; a convincing force

When it comes to Authority, you will define the authority levels for your team which will allow them to make the right decisions or to direct others when it comes to them making the right decisions. When you give your team the authority to make decisions, you are fully empowering them to be successful. When you push the decision-making process down to your team members, you are making them feel as if they part of a team and once again not just a number. Through authority, you are setting:

- The stage where they now have legitimate power.
- The stage to where they will become leaders themselves.
- Up the right targets and expectations for your team.
- Up the right environment for your team.

This helps complete the trust level you want to have with your team.

Authority must be clear to the individual and the team. Team members will operate best when their individual levels of authority match their individual responsibilities. Authority comes down to the ability to make decisions. When defining the authority levels for your team, it is important to know who controls what within the decision-making process. When it comes to decision-making, you will discover that there may be "many bosses" within the team or institutional structure. It will be up to you as a leader to define your team's decision-making capabilities and what they actually own. Your team members will need to know who they need to talk to, when they need to talk to them and how communication between the teams will be conducted when it comes to the decision-making process. Using EEI will help in the decision-making process.

Where your team does not have control of the decision making, it will be you and your team's responsibility to hold the outside decision makers accountable for the decisions they make when it comes to your team process or customer deliverables. This is especially true when a manager outside of your team controls their own team's decision-making capabilities. This manager can include an internal or external partner, a supplier to your institution or an internal or external institutional team leader outside of your organization.

Each team member will have different levels of authority in the decision-making process. This can also be the same levels of responsibility and accountability each team member controls or owns. Your job guidelines and task lists will help define the "RAA" for each of your team members.

Problem Solving, Negotiation and Conflict Management

President John Adams said: "Every problem is an opportunity in disguise." Through your problem solving, negotiation and conflict management processes, become aware of these opportunities and take advantage of them as they appear to your team.

When it comes to your team's decision-making process, problems can arise that will need to be addressed. This will require some level of negotiation between your team and the decision makers. Albert Einstein said: "The significant problems we face cannot be solved at the same level of thinking we were at when we created them." Enter your problem solving and negotiation with an open, non-biased mind. When you start your problem-solving exercise:

- You will need to clearly define the problem first which can be done via a problem statement.
- Analysis of the problem will be conducted and alternatives will be discussed to help the decision makers come up with a solution to the problem.

When it comes to conflict resolution, you have a variety of options available to you to manage their outcome. You can:

- Confront the problem via problem solving.
- Come to some level of compromise between the teams that have the conflict.
- Avoid the problem and hope it goes away.
- Try to "smooth over" the team that has the problem.
- Force a solution, even though everyone may not agree on the solution.

As experience goes, problem solving is the best solution for all teams involved. And finally, when it comes to problem solving; get and stay involved, take responsibility, be part of the solution and not part of the problem.

Tying it together, Power and RAA

When we look at Power, you are letting your team know that the "The Buck stops here" as President Harry S. Truman would say, when it comes time for you and your team to lead. When you tie together Responsibility, Accountability and Authority, you are telling your team they are a valuable part of your institution. The team members:

- Are empowered.
- Have the power to make decisions.
- Are reliable and entrusted to make decisions.
- Are in control and take ownership in the decisions they make.
- Have the ability to be a leader for the team process elements that they actually own.
- Have the ability to lead others on decisions out of their control.
- Hold the outside decision makers accountable for their own actions and decisions when it comes to your team and to your customer.

Remember, an effective leader has the ability to influence others into doing something they normally would not do on their own. By empowering your team, you will become an effective leader along with teaching them how to become effective leaders themselves. Being "just a number" is removed from your team and your team process.

Expanded Power and RAA Table Summary

Building your team	• Power, Motivation and People along with taking the initiative
• Power	• Empowerment through mutual respect and trust • Allow your team to take control and be in charge by taking ownership • Tie back to your repeatable team process • Set realistic targets and provide meaningful direction • Set up the right working environment

• Responsibility	•	Respect and trust your team
	•	Define team roles and responsibilities
	•	Define their core competencies in the job guidelines
	•	Define their secondary job functions via task lists
	•	Do both with clarity and focus
	•	Define job functions and tasks that have meaning, provide direction and are easy to understand
	•	Tie back to your repeatable team process
	•	Be SMART, Use EEI and The 5 Whys
• Accountability	•	Define areas of accountability
	•	Define ownership levels
	•	Be engaged with your team
	•	Set an open team agenda
	•	Set decision making levels
	•	Make accountability part of your team culture
	•	Integrate and communicate
• Authority	•	Define and set authority levels for decision making
	•	Use EEI
	•	Empowerment through mutual respect and trust
	•	Define team targets
	•	Set team expectations for hitting their targets
	•	Create the right environment
	•	Problem solve

Self-directed Power and RAA

While the focus on this book is effective leadership when it comes to Power, it may be important to understand the 7 types of Power an individual may possess. This should help you when it comes to defining the steps you may want to take for self-directed power. The 7 types of Individual or Self-directed Power are:

- Legitimate Power – Where power is given to you based on the position you hold. It can be considered the same as team or organizational power or via a chain-of-command type of structure.
- Referent Power – Being accepted or gaining approval through positive influence. Considered the most valuable type of power. One can gain respect with their peers and the leaders in their institution with this type of power. This type of power is where "Attitude reflects leadership" comes into play.
- Expert Power – This power is based on your skills and what you know, especially when it comes to leading people. It is knowledge-based and can be enhanced through continually learning.
- Information Power – Information is power. Most good Project Managers possess this power type and it is extremely effective when leading successful product or project teams.
- Reward Power – Motivating others through rewards and recognition.
- Connection Power – Networking with successful and powerful people. Politics are sometimes involved with this power type.
- Coercive Power – Where a person leads via threats or use of force. Being an institutional or corporate bully. It is the least effective type of "Power" leadership. You cannot become trustworthy or build credibility with your team using this power type.

Cartman from Comedy Central's television show, _South Park_ is a prime example of someone practicing coercive power with his attitude and catchphrase of "Respect my Authoritah!" when it comes time for Cartman to lead. Coercive power is also saved for last to elaborate on why it does not work when it comes to leading a team. With some teams, there are certain team environments where a few "so-called Bosses" lead through coercive power and behavior. The "Bosses" on these teams feel that bully tactics through intimidation, fear and submission are the best ways to lead a team. They do not understand that mutual respect and trust between themselves and their team members is what is really needed when it comes to leading a successful team.

As stated before, respect and trust, rather than intimidation, fear and submission, are the key elements of effective leadership. When using coercive power, your team, at the bare minimum, will perform their duties but it is guaranteed that you will not gain their respect or trust. In most environments, coercive power does not work well as most employees do not have a contractual obligation that keeps them in their job. You can leave the job if you don't like, trust or even respect the boss. This is especially true if they are an institutional or corporate bully.

Now back to self-directed power. Choose the correct power-type that fits your situational needs. Do not become an institutional or corporate bully. Do not become a Cartman. Follow Aesop's example where persuasion wins over force when it comes to leading your team.

- Become an effective leader by empowering yourself based on the job or task you are entrusted to perform.
- Prove to everyone that you are reliable when performing your job or your task.
- Lead by example. Set the example.
- Take control and be in charge by taking ownership through knowing what you are responsible and accountable for within your team process.
- Do not be afraid when it comes to making the right team decisions and hold the outside decisions makers accountable for their own decisions, their own actions.
- And finally, know how to effectively solve problems and provide solutions and do so as soon as the problem presents itself to your team.

Motivation – Power, Achievement, Affiliation

Building your team	• Power, Motivation and People along with taking the initiative
• Motivation	• Power – Empowerment through mutual respect and trust • Achievement – Through accomplishment, through recognition and reward • Affiliation – A sense of belonging, a sense of community

<u>Motivation</u> - a motivating force, stimulus or influence; incentive; driven

Motivation comes in many forms and has been written about for many years. President Dwight D. Eisenhower said: "Motivation is the art of getting people to do what you want them to do because they want to do it." When it comes to team motivation, it is your job as a leader to:

- Set the direction and the proper expectations for your team built on the mutual respect and trust you have put in place so that your team is motivated to do their best.
- Ask for and then encourage from your team members their feedback along with anyone else's feedback that has an interest in what your team does when providing the direction and setting the expectations for your team.
- Understand that the expectations which have been set for your team, the team process which have been put in place for your team are dynamic and open to change. Do not create the team process in a vacuum or a silo where there has been no team input, where it is inflexible and not open to change.

- Take control and be in charge when setting the expectations for your team based on the feedback you receive from your team or anyone else that has a vested interest in your team process.
- Not force people to work based only on inflexible expectations and / or static controls when it comes to your team.
- Stay away from the "Boss" or Yes Man" process structure for your team.

If given the right environment, your team members will become what you want them to be, members of an outstanding team. Open communication, teamwork and team member empowerment through responsibility, accountability and authority can help in setting up the right team environment.

Frederic Herzburg's Theory of Hygiene Factors – A Business Application

Frederic Herzburg's Theory of Hygiene Factors, along with Bernard Mausner and Barbara Block Snyderman broke out motivation by satisfiers and dissatisfiers.

Motivating Agents that can act as a dissatisfier.	Motivating Agents that can act as a satisfier.
• Company policies and administration • Supervision • Salary • Interpersonal relationships at work • Working conditions • Personal life • Job security	• Achievement • Recognition • Work itself • Responsibility • Advancement • Self-actualization

While everyone early on in the field of motivation considered salary as a non-motivator, it is still very important to compensate your team members accordingly based on the job responsibilities they have along with the talent they bring to your team. If you don't compensate them properly, they will eventually leave your team for better opportunities and greener pastures.

- Provide your team good working conditions.
- Build and maintain a positive working environment.

- Provide a good work / life balance. Remember "All work and no play makes Jack a very dull boy."
- Provide them the security and status they deserve.
- Recognize team and individual achievements and continue to develop and grow your team through excellent leadership, coaching, mentoring and training.

When it comes to coaching, Susan Peters said: "The wonderful thing about positive coaching is that people can lean into things they are already good at and do even better."

- Encourage active participation from all your team members.
- Maintain open communication, encourage team feedback and be an active listener.
- Allow your team to reach self-actualization.
- Understand and fulfill their wishes where you are allowed.

Abraham Maslow's Hierarchy of Human Needs

Abraham Maslow's Hierarchy of Human Needs provided a top-to-bottom type of structure for motivation. From top-to-bottom they are:

- Self-actualization (top)
- Esteem
- Love (Social)
- Safety
- Physiological (bottom)

According to Abraham Maslow, your goal and your team's goal is to reach the top motive within his hierarchy. When a team member reaches Self-actualization, they are at the point where they feel that nothing can hold them back and they can accomplish anything that is presented to them as an individual or as a member of a successful team. Abraham Maslow said: "The classifications of motivation must be based on goals." These goals are the same goals which have been set for your team. Abraham went on to say: "An organized world is what your team needs rather than an unorganized or unstructured one." Managing your team through your team process provides you the organization you need. And finally, Abraham said: "A healthy man is primarily motivated by his needs to develop and to actualize his fullest potential and capacity."

David McClelland's Motives

David McClelland's work in motivation is what is referenced to define the Motivation and PAA building block in this section of the book. David said: "Motives drive, orient and select behavior." This behavior can be at the individual level or the team level. Nothing is taken away from what David created. No credit is taken away from his outstanding work. The motivation-based information contained in this book is presented to you in a way that allows you to motivate your team through positive re-enforcement, creating the team you will want to lead. You can use David's work to further build your team's foundation.

When criticism is provided to your team or directed at a team member, it should be provided in a constructive way. By motivating your team in a positive way, they will respond better to constructive criticism and not feel broken down through which destructive criticism can bring. This keeps your team motivated to deliver great results.

When David developed his motives, he looked at them as something that is developed through time, through your own work and even your own life experiences. He looked at the motives where one motive may become more dominant over the other motives as you progress through life. It is generally thought that you as a leader will understand the dominant motive for your team members and you will know how to use these motives to influence your team when setting the goals for your team.

Motivation is the second part of your foundation building blocks which contains the next three important parts – PAA. PAA is Power, Achievement and Affiliation. David first defined the PAA motives at the individual level. The definition of his work is an outstanding model to follow and will be used as the basis when defining the PAA motives as they apply to leading your team at the team level.

Power - ability to act or produce an effect; possession of control, authority or influence over others

The Power motive as mentioned before in the Power section of this book is empowering your team to being successful. It is giving them the responsibility and accountability they want and need along with the authority they need for making the right decisions. It shows that you:

- Respect and trust them when they take control and are in charge by taking ownership of the things they own within your team process.
- Can rely on them for getting the job done.

David McClelland and the Power Motive

When David defined the Power motive, it was what a true leader represents. They are someone that likes to influence others. They are goal-oriented, they like to win and they enjoy the competition that comes with winning. They are someone that looks to take charge and be in control of their own destiny. They enjoy the status of what it takes to being on a winning team and what a winning team can bring. As stated before by William Jennings Bryan and in the movie *Caddy Shack*, "Destiny is not by chance, but by choice"; "See your future, be your future." Make the right choices when it comes to your own destiny and the destiny of others around you. When it comes to your future and the future of others around you.

Achievement - a result gained by effort; a great or heroic deed; accomplishment

The Achievement motive comes from team accomplishments. When it comes to effective leadership, Peter Block said: "People matter. They are not just a means to an end. Relationships are the foundation for accomplishment." Because literally everyone wants to have a good experience, you will want to set-up your team to accomplish great things.

As stated before, the first step is through empowerment. The second step is creating team-building relationships through trust, open communication and mutual respect, key components of empowerment. Empowering your team to being successful in a positive way will bring meaningful results to your team and the team relationships they build.

David looked at strong achievers and the Achievement motive as being the most important motive when it came to a team. When your team accomplishes what you want and not only meets but beats your expectations, RECOGNIZE THEM AND REWARD THEM. A prime example of recognition and reward comes from Tom Izzo, Head Coach of the Michigan State University Men's Basketball Team. When his team won the 2000 NCAA Men's Basketball Championship, he rewarded every member of his staff, to include his Secretary and Janitor, a championship ring. By Coach Izzo doing this, he let every member of his staff know that they are an integral part of his team's success and without their efforts his team would not have been as successful as they were. Be a "Coach Izzo." Let every member of your team know that you appreciate their efforts and what they do for you, your team and your customer. It can be "You did a good job" or as easy and simple as a "Thank You." It also does not hurt to celebrate their success. A good party to celebrate their success and your team's success is always appreciated by all.

David McClelland and the Achievement Motive

When we look at David's Achievement motive, when it comes to being a strong achiever, we see someone that lives for the challenge. They are task-oriented and are willing to take moderate calculated risks when it comes to accomplishing the task. They are a strong believer in the importance of what feedback and positive re-enforcement represents and they always look for areas of self-improvement. They are also someone that typically prefers to work alone. David believed that strong achievers are also representative of what it takes to be successful in business and they have the competitive entrepreneurial spirit required of successful people. The strong achievers are, in fact, a key factor in the economic growth of the business. David also believed that achieving the goal and successfully completing complex tasks were more important to a strong achiever than what monetary recognition could bring.

__Affiliation__ - to associate as a member; to bring or receive into close connection as a member; to connect or associate oneself; combine

Through the Affiliation motive, everyone wants to be on a winning team. When setting up your team, following the team dynamics of Forming, Storming, Norming and Performing can help you in your initial team set-up if you have not done so already. Setting your team up for success puts them on the winning side of things and the results you receive from their success are immeasurable. You will see it in the attitude of your team, how they carry themselves and their camaraderie towards one another.

As stated before "Attitude reflects leadership." Set the "right attitude" for your team by being a leader. Lead by example. Set the example. When your team walks the halls of your institution, they will hold their heads up high showing the confidence, "the attitude", you want to see from your team. They will connect with each other well along with showing others the confidence a winning team possesses. Being on a winning team gives them a sense of belonging, a sense of community, which is something no one can take away from them, EVER.

David McClelland and the Affiliation Motive

David's work with people with strong Affiliation traits was more about the individual and how a strong affiliation was important to them for a sense of belonging. They are comfortable being part of a team, over the more individualistic traits which a strong Power motive or a strong Achievement motive type of individual may possess. They tend to avoid conflict and prefer feedback for how well the team is getting along and performing rather than how well they are performing individually. They prefer collaboration over competition and are not big risk takers. To get to this level along with being on a winning team requires a good playbook which everyone likes and agrees on.

Your well-documented team process is your playbook. It contains the EEI for your success and provides the right direction and the right environment for your team. As mentioned before, a well-defined team process is where your team is on-board. Having a well-documented team process for your team to follow and utilizing the team dynamic principles, will take you to where you want to go when it comes to the success of your team along with the success of delivering a high-quality product to your customer.

Tying it together, Motivation and PAA

Tying it together, the second part of your foundation's building block, PAA. A motivated team is a well-oiled machine, running on all cylinders. They:

- Are empowered, accomplishing great things and are part of a winning team which is based on trust, open communication and mutual respect.
- Want to get things done and are not afraid of getting their hands dirty or their feet wet.
- Are in charge and taking control of their own destiny based on the direction set for them.
- Understand the importance of positive feedback and use it to its fullest potential.

When things do get a little tough, which at times they will, they will know how to handle the situation and will respond in the way you expect them to. They are:

- Willing, ready and able to step in and make the situation right so that your team can deliver a high-quality product to your customer.
- Positive and driven to succeed.

Expanded Motivation and PAA Table Summary

Building your team	
	• Power, Motivation and People along with taking the initiative
• Motivation	• Allow your team to take control and be in charge by taking ownership • Set the proper expectations and create the right working environment • Practice positive motivation and constructive criticism
• Power	• Empowerment through mutual respect and trust • Allow your team to take control and be in charge by taking ownership • Tie back to your repeatable team process • Set realistic targets and provide meaningful direction • Set up the right working environment
• Achievement	• Empowerment through mutual respect and trust • Team-building relationships • Recognize and reward • Provide positive re-enforcement and feedback

• Affiliation	• Attitude reflects leadership • Lead by example, set the example • Tie back to your repeatable team process • Create the right environment • A sense of belonging, a sense of community

Self-directed Motivation and PAA

For self-directed motivation, what do you do? Well for one, if you don't know ASK! Perform the following:

- Empower yourself. Find out what you are empowered to do, then go out and do it.
- Have the strength and the discipline to motivate yourself to be successful.
- Be in control of your own destiny and take aim at your own targets and the targets set for you from your leadership team.
- Take charge and make things happen.
- Challenge yourself and others around you.
- Make sure you have the right tools and processes in place to accomplish the things you are entrusted to perform and do so with the utmost level of integrity and quality and then hit your targets, your deliverables, as others may be dependent on you and your deliverables to them.
- Recognize the achievements of others on your team and let them know you appreciate their efforts and their accomplishments. Once again, a simple "You did a good job" and "Thank You" can go a long way.
- Be an active listener and always provide timely positive feedback to your team members.
- Stay driven and positive.
- Maintain a positive attitude for your team. Be a positive influence and role model to your teammates.
- Lead by example. Set the example.

Through positive influence and being a role model to your team, your teammates can trust knowing that when it really comes down to it, you will cover their backs when they need it and they will reciprocate the same for you when it is required.

People – Talent, Experience, Technique

Building your team	• Power, Motivation and People along with taking the initiative
• People	• Talent – Knowing Strengths, Weaknesses, Opportunities and Threats through SWOT Analysis, "SO EASE into it...." • Experience – The "right" experience vs. the "wrong" experience • Technique – Process, SWOT Analysis, "WhaT's the MATA...."

People - human beings making up a group or assembly or linked by a common interest

As stated before at the start of this book is the quote from General Colin Powell on People and leadership. "Leadership is all about people. It is not about organizations. It is not about plans. It is not about strategies. It is all about people motivating people to get the job done. You have to be people-centered." Remember that people are your greatest asset, your most important commodity. If your team process and individual team resources are not properly led or aligned, there will competition between all the teams all vying for the same resources which can have a negative impact to your customer. You as a leader are only as good as the people on your team. It is up to you as a leader at making your team be the best they can be, and as it has been said before, the RAA, PAA, TET principles can help make this happen.

It has been said that Alexander the Great knew his men by their first names. Get to know your team. Operate as a team. Know each team member's unique creative talents and abilities, their core competencies and where team members may be considered weak in an area, TRAIN THEM. Investments in training are strategic bets in your people.

Training also enables your people in ways you may not have experienced as the future belongs to those who keep learning and have an incessant drive to search for what is new. Know that people are unique individuals. Know that a lesson plan for one person may not work for another and the lesson plan may have to be modified to fit the person and their individual training needs. When the right people come together, once again, they will accomplish great things and when you are motivating them the right way they will perform the way you expect them to perform and beyond.

When tying your team members back to your team process, once again it is important to know that business and team processes are collaborative. They involve people. Through this collaboration of processes, you are setting your people up where they share a common interest or goal. This will come:

- From your well-documented team process.
- YOU and your ability to lead your team.
- YOU taking charge and leading your team.

SWOT Analysis; Strength, Weakness, Opportunity and Threat.

A tool to assist you in getting the most out of your people is following the acronym used to strengthen your team – SWOT. SWOT is Strength, Weakness, Opportunity and Threat. In project management, it is used in assessing risk or risk management analysis and it can also be used to build a really strong team. Through SWOT:

- Risk assessment and analysis is responding to a changing environment that can affect your team.
- Understanding your team environment and their abilities helps your team handle any type of risky scenario they may experience.
- It provides the tools your team needs for handling the risky scenario extremely well.

Great books on People

There have been some great books written on "People" and how to lead people. Where you can, obtain a copy of these books and read them.

Stephen Covey's Habit 6, Synergize

From Stephen Covey's book, *The 7 Habits of Highly Effective People: Powerful Lessons in Personal Change* there are 7 habits which improve your ability at leading people which we have already referenced in previous sections of this book. Another one is Habit 6, Synergize. It is very good for when leading and dealing with people. Stephen said: "Synergize is combining the strengths of people through positive teamwork, so as to achieve goals no one person could have done on their own. The essence of synergy is to value differences – to respect them; to build on strengths, to compensate weaknesses." This is being a leader. Remember, a leader is someone that has the ability to influence others into doing something they normally would not do on their own. Work to change your team member's attitude in a positive way.

Stephen went on to say, "When one works on attitude, nothing can be a hindrance to one's effectiveness in life. Synergy works and the end result when it comes to synergy are where new goals, shared goals are created, and the whole enterprise moves forward, often in ways no one could have anticipated. The excitement contained within that movement creates a new culture where people are empowered by new, fresh thinking, by new creative alternatives and opportunities." As stated before, remember, "One's own destiny is by choice." "See your future, Be your future." "Attitude reflects leadership."

William "Bill" Walton's book *The New Bottom Line*

William "Bill" Walton was one of the co-founders of Holiday Inn Hotels. In his book's introduction he talked about some really good phrases he found to be very beneficial when leading and dealing with people.

Bill Walton's Short Course in Human Relations

There are six phrases which are a "Short course in Human Relations." The six most important words in Human Relations are….

- "I admit I made a mistake"

The five most important words….

- 'You did a good job"

The four most important words….

- "What is your opinion?"

The three most important words....

- "If you please"

The two most important words....

- "Thank You"

The most important word....

- "We"

The least important word....

- "I"

The six phrases from Bill Walton show that you have the confidence to take action when it comes to leading a team and you are willing to make the tough decisions that need to be made to properly lead a team. Understanding and following these phrases also show that you are part of a team. There is nothing elaborate about these phrases and they are extremely effective when followed. These phrases allow you to challenge your team, to understand and take calculated risks for being successful by letting your team know that anyone can make a mistake and that you want them to try without the fear of failing. They are willing to explore unchartered territory by taking on the risk at being successful.

And when it comes to risks, here are some additional quotes on risk taking that are really good when it comes to dealing with human relations. General Patton said: "Take calculated risks. That is quite different from being rash." Frederick Wilcox said: "Progress always involves risks. You can't steal second base and keep your foot on first." President Jimmy Carter said: "Go out on a limb. That's where the fruit is." President Franklin D. Roosevelt in his 1st Inaugural speech said: "The only thing we have to fear is fear itself." Michael Jordan said: "I have failed many times, that is why I succeed." An old Latin Proverb states: "Fortune favors the bold." And finally, Norman Vincent Peale said: "Action is a great restorer and builder of confidence. Inaction is not only the result, but the cause, of fear. Perhaps the action you take will be successful; perhaps different action or adjustments will have to follow. But any action is better than no action at all." Team success requires action. Inaction and indecisiveness on your part or your team's part leads to:

- Uncertainty and causes delays in your process.
- A lack of or a loss of confidence from your team when it comes to you leading your team.

This inaction and indecisiveness can come from a poorly defined team process. Mistakes can be eliminated or reduced with a well-defined team process. When it came to mistakes, Henry Ford said: "The only real mistake is the one from which we learn nothing." Mistakes can be fixed and once again it is okay to take some calculated risks and to make some mistakes along the way as long as we fix them and learn from them so as not to repeat them the next go around. The six phrases from Bill Walton also show:

- You appreciate your team and their efforts through praise.
- You value and trust your teams' opinion.
- You treat them with respect.
- You give them a sense of belonging, a sense of community. They belong to a team. YOUR TEAM.
- When "We" operate as a team, there is nothing "We" cannot do.
- There is no "I" in team.

Dale Carnegie's Principle # 1

In Dale's book, *How to Win Friends and Influence People* he talks about some negative behaviors that can be detrimental to your team. These behaviors will act as an inhibitor to your team's success and should be avoided. These behaviors make up Dale's Principle # 1 of "Don't criticize, condemn or complain." Dale Carnegie references several renowned psychologists where he said: "Criticism is futile because it puts a person on the defensive and usually makes him strive to justify himself. Criticism is dangerous, because it wounds a person's precious pride, hurts his sense of importance, and arouses resentment. By criticizing, we do not make lasting changes and often incur resentment. The resentment that criticism engenders can demoralize employees, family members and friends, and still not correct the situation that has been condemned."

When you look at criticism, stay away from negative criticism which can be construed as a personal attack. Also understand that constructive criticism can be beneficial to your team. When constructive criticism is given make sure it is provided in a timely manner. Don't wait two to three months to provide it, be very specific in your discussion with your team member when you do provide it and finally allow your team member time to provide their feedback based on your discussion with them. Out of constructive criticism, improvements can be made which your team or a team member can benefit from. Understand and know the difference between negative criticism and constructive criticism.

When it comes to condemning people, it is better to understanding them first before you condemn them. As Dale said: "God himself, sir, does not propose to judge man until his end of days." Based on this statement, it is not our place to condemn our fellow man or woman. And finally, don't openly complain where others can hear your complaints. Complaining in itself is enough to bring a team down even if the other 2 behaviors are not present. Besides, President Theodore Roosevelt said: "Complaining about a problem without proposing a solution is called whining." Don't be a complainer. Don't be a whiner.

Good "C" Words

A number of negative words that begin with "C" have been presented. Now think of some good "C" words that can be positive and extremely beneficial to your team. There are a lot of good "C" words.

These include Communication, Clear, Concise, Commodity, Collaboration, Cultivate, Cooperation, Coordination, Compatible, Cohesion, Consistent, Connect, Contribution, Chemistry, Camaraderie, Compromise, Commitment, Competent, Confident, Control, Charge, Context, Concentrate, Clarity, Compelling, Character, Culture, Challenge, Courage, Create, Celebrate and finally Ceremony. Through your own experiences you will be able to define some more good "C" words which your team can benefit from.

Your team should always maintain open communication within and outside of your team. They become active listeners. Let your team know that they can openly communicate up and down the chain-of-command and once again that their opinion means something to you and brings value. Also maintain open communication with your customer to build a good working relationship and to maintain the level of respect and trust you and your customer have both come to expect. As the saying goes "Information is power." You cannot have power if you don't share valuable information through open communication. When it comes to communicating with your team, don't be a wimp. Be clear and concise in the communication to your team. Be straight forward with your team. Ask direct and straight forward questions to your team and expect direct and straight forward answers from them.

Another reference on the value information brings comes from Oliver Stone's movie *Wall Street*. In the movie, Gordon Gekko says that the most valuable commodity is information. Your team members cannot perform their jobs effectively without access to the information needed to do their job. Gordon also looked at information as being extremely valuable where good decisions can be made. Also remember this as stated before, one of your most important commodities are your people, your greatest asset. Treat your people well.

From the Microsoft Surface commercial, "For any player, for any coach, for any team, the art of collaboration builds champions, it empowers us all." Collaborate internally within your institutional teams and externally with your external partners and your customer to build your championship team.

Cultivate and don't alienate. Build relationships internally and externally. Let your team know that an effective team requires the cooperation from all team members and not just from a select few. Let your team know that their coordinated efforts create a positive workflow to their work; the things they are working on; trying to accomplish, which will be finished in a timely manner through their coordinated efforts where they deliver a quality product to your customer.

A team should be a compatible and cohesive unit, consistently working together, able to connect with one another for the betterment of the team and your customer. Patrick Lencioni stated how teammates on truly cohesive teams behave. They:

- Trust one another.
- Engage in unfiltered conflict around ideas.
- Commit to decisions and plans of action.
- Hold one another accountable for delivering against those plans.
- Focus on the achievement of collective results.

When everyone contributes to the team effort their contributions lead to delivering a high-quality product to your customer. And through time, with their connections and contributions, along with working as a cohesive team, there is a certain level of team chemistry that is developed within the team. The right amount of team chemistry where there is team camaraderie after the product delivery or the project is complete. A little give and take is sometimes required to getting things done so you have to be willing to compromise to make sure the team effort and productive progress continues.

When it comes to commitment, Margaret Mead said: "Never doubt that a small group of thoughtful, committed people can change the world. Indeed it is the only thing that ever has." Howard Schultz said: "When you are surrounded by people who share a passionate commitment around a common purpose, anything is possible." Peter Drucker said: "Unless commitment is made, there are only promises and hope, but no plans." Be committed to what you and your team are doing. Gain approval, buy-in and sign-off based on the commitments you receive. Communicate and make it aware to everyone what your level of commitment is to the team, your mission and your customer deliverables. As a leader, show your team that you are committed to the team's success. Self-interests or hidden agendas do nothing for team morale. It only shows that you are not committed to the team and only are looking to taking care of yourself first.

Stay competent. Always keep learning new ways for doing things to make yourself and your team better. Stay confident. Continually play up to your own strengths to deliver a high-quality product to your customer. Muhammed Ali said: "It's not bragging if you can back it up."

Be in Control and Take Charge

Be in control when it comes to:

- Leading your team, supporting your team and your customer.
- Dealing with outside decision makers and holding the outside decision makers accountable for their own actions.
- Your own destiny. Take aim of your targets. Don't just sit back and depend on others to do things for you, especially when it is your job to getting it done.
- Taking charge of your team and your support groups. Show everyone that you know what it takes to be an effective leader.
- Staying within context. Be clear and concise in what you and your team need to do.

During the 2016 Ryder Cup, professional golfer and the US Ryder Cup Team Coach Davis Love III asked Coach Bill Belichick (Head Coach of the New England Patriots) how he should prepare his players to win the Ryder Cup. Bill told Davis to have his players to "Concentrate on your job, do your job." This same level of concentration goes back to what Drew Brees' said, where your teammates focus on the same goal. That the level of focus and concentration from your team goes back to the "must have" customer deliverables, your customers' expectations. Make sure you define the team, product or project requirements with enough clarity that they are easily understood by everyone. Make the compelling argument for what you believe in which is your team and your team process.

Your character says a lot about you. Your character builds trust. And when it comes to character, an excellent example comes from Theo Epstein, the President of the Chicago Cubs. Theo looks for players that have strong character traits and they have the ability to handle and deal with adversity when it appears. When it comes to you and your team, have "Strength in Character." Make sure you possess the right character traits and that you look to instill the right character traits into your team. Edgar Schein said: "Culture is to a group what personality or character is to an individual. Just as our personality and character guide and constrain our behavior, so does culture guide and constrain the behavior of members of a group through the shared norms that are held in that group." No different than your own character, develop the right culture for your team. If done properly, it creates the shared community for which your team will thrive to belong to. Also understand the importance of cultural diversity and inclusion along how your team can benefit from the two. Cultural diversity and inclusion can help bring a different view or perspective in how we do things.

Lead by example. Set the example. Challenge yourself. Challenge your team. Take on the challenge for building your team through RAA, PAA, TET. Overcome the challenges you may face when you build your team. Challenge your team to be the best they can be at everything they do.

From the old CBS show *Cheers and the episode, A Bar is Born*, Sam Malone is talking to Robin Colcord about a new bar he bought after he had sold his bar, Cheers to Robin's company. In the discussion, Robin let Sam know one of the things that makes him successful. Robin told Sam that: "The secret to success is having a dream and having the courage to run after it. Reach for the stars." Steve Jobs said: "Have the courage to follow your heart and intuition. They somehow already know what you truly want to become. Everything else is secondary."

Steve Jobs went on to say: "People with passion can change the world for the better." Muhammed Ali said: "He who is not courageous enough to take risks will accomplish nothing in life." And finally, when it comes to courage, in the movie *Braveheart*, Sir William Wallace tells Earl the Bruce that: "Men won't follow titles, Men follow courage." Don't be a coward. Have the courage to step up, to lead your team the way they deserve to be led when it comes to them being successful. Have the courage to step up and get it done when you challenge yourself and your team.

Be creative when getting it done. Have the discipline and patience to getting it done and getting it done right. Don't settle for second best and don't wait for someone else to do it for you. Remember Rome was not built in a day and neither will your team and their team process. And finally, with the Good "C" Words, don't be afraid to celebrate your team's success. Create a little fanfare and ceremony when celebrating your team's success.

What it takes to be a Really Good Team Leader or Member

In the past, there have been a lot of articles written about the disengaged team member along with the qualities that are deemed important for being a team leader along with what it takes to be a really good team member. Some of the top qualities of a really good team leader or team member that consistently come up are:

- Having the ability to lead.
- Having a strong understanding of what it takes to be part of a team. The value of being part of the team, part of a community.
- Knowing that diversity, inclusion and interpersonal skills are important when it comes to being part of the team.
- That in order to be successful requires teamwork and active participation from all the members of the team.
- They are customer focused.
- They are committed to the team vision.
- They are open to others' ideas.
- They have the ability to think on their own.
- They can address and solve problems.
- They are independent, imaginative, creative and critical thinkers.
- They know how to deal with adversity.
- They are confident in their abilities and the abilities of the team.
- They know the importance of networking and communicating along with the types of communication to use; formal and informal, direct and indirect, when dealing with all situations as they appear.
- They are active listeners. They learn to listen and listen to learn.
- And finally, when you find a top leader or performer that has these qualities, use them. Put them in the game. Don't leave them on the bench.

This leads us to our final building block; People. People bring us to the third part of your foundation building blocks which contains the next three important parts – TET. TET is Talent, Experience and Technique.

Talent - the natural endowments of a person; general intelligence or mental power; ability

The show _Everyone Got's Talent_ could not be further from the truth. Everyone is good at something in one way or another. Some people are just naturally talented. From the book _Talent Wins_ by Ram Charan, Dominic Barton and Dennis Carey, they state that: "Talent is the value creator. Talented people are innovative, they get to the heart of the issues, they reframe ideas, they create informal bonds that encourage collaboration and they make the team healthier and more productive."

The "SO" of SWOT

It has been said that while Rudy Giuliani was the Mayor of New York City, he would fill his staff positions with people that were strong in an area he was weak in. These people were talented experts in their field and helped to strengthen the Mayor's office. Talent is a strength and opportunity (SO) for your team to use and capitalize on. Michael Jordan said: "Talent wins games, but teamwork and intelligence wins championships." Babe Ruth said: "The way a team plays as a whole determines its success. You may have the greatest bunch of individual stars in the world, but if they don't play together, the club won't be worth a dime." It is your job to make sure your talented team members play as a team. Talent brings a creative mind-set to your team. Your team's creative talents along with their core competencies should be used to their fullest potential. Use the individual talent each team member brings and tie it together through teamwork and the principles of RAA, PAA, TET for your team's success.

For all your team's strengths and opportunities, you will use the acronym, EASE. An easy way to remember this acronym as it relates to positive SWOT analysis is through a simple sentence of "SO, we will EASE into what we want and need to do" or simply put "SO, let's EASE into it." EASE represents – Enhance, Accept, Share and Exploit in the positive aspects of SWOT analysis. By "EASE'ing" into your team's strength's you are taking the opportunity for empowering and improving your team. You will:

- Enhance their creative talents by providing additional training for your talented team members to make them even better.
- Accept and recognize their creative talents because not doing so simply does not make much sense.
- Share this creative talent by where your talented individuals can share and teach others in the techniques they use that enhance their own particular talent.
- Exploit these creative talents giving your team members the freedom to use their talents when they are needed within your team process and your team.

If you don't empower, recognize, accept and use your talented team members, you stand to leave their creative talents "on the bench". And, if you are not careful, or even worst, they will leave your team by being under-utilized. Put your creative talented people in:

- A position to succeed.
- The game and let them play through the freedom which empowerment will bring to your team.

By "EASE'ing" into what you need to do, you remove most of the risk that could get in your way for your team being successful.

Experience - practical knowledge, skill or practice derived from direct observation of or participation in events or in a particular activity

When it comes to experience and skill, David Starr Jordan said: "Wisdom is knowing what to do next, skill is knowing how to do it, and virtue is doing it." Aristotle said: "We are what we repeatedly do. Excellence, then, is not an act, but a habit." Stephen Covey said: "We define a habit as the intersection of knowledge, skill and desire. Knowledge is the *what to do* and the *why*. Skill is the *how to do*. Desire is the motivation, the *want to do*." When it comes to your people and your team process, make it to where they "Become a creature of habit." This comes from your well-defined "repeatable" team process which becomes a "habit" for your people to follow. Oscar Wilde said: "Experience is the one thing you can't get for nothing." Experience comes from doing. It does not come from doing nothing. It comes from:

- The experience your team gains from your people performing their jobs repeatedly based on the team process you put in place.
- Empowerment and active participation from your team members.

Your team member cannot gain "game-time experience" if you do not put them in the game. Experience allows your team members to get better at their core competencies. Put them in the game, let them play and learn from your good active coaching.

Where the product or project delivery to your customer allows, make sure you cross-train your team members and then rotate your team members through a coordinated effort so that they can gain the experience they need to be successful. When you put into action a well-defined consistent and repeatable team process, your team will work in the right environment and gain the "right" experience needed to be successful. A poorly defined or even a poorly designed team process brings no value to you or your team.

With a poorly defined team process in place, your team will be in the wrong environment and gain the "wrong" experience. It leads to inconsistency, ambiguity and uncertainty within your team and loss in your team's confidence. Understanding your team process and providing the proper tools will enhance your team's experience. Equip your team with the best tools possible.

Empowering your team members allows them to gain experience. By empowering your people with a well-defined team process, you will give them the "right" fundamental experience they need to apply everything they learn from you. Through experience, sometimes there are mistakes that are made. Correct them and then learn from them. Let your people know that:

- Everyone makes mistakes.
- Mistakes are allowed and that we learn from them and improve based on the experience, so the next time the situation presents itself they will know how to deal with it and will not repeat the same mistake twice.

Technique - a method of accomplishing a desired aim

Technique and experience are extremely inter-related as technique teaches us the process for doing things and how we accomplish key tasks; while experience teaches us how to apply what we learned and how to motivate people to successfully achieve those tasks. Technique is something that is taught. Technique starts at teaching your team fundamentals to your team. Just make sure you are teaching your team the "right" team process. A process that is fundamentally sound, consistent and repeatable.

- Aim your team in right direction.

- Take control and provide your team the direction needed for them to be successful.
- Make sure your team members can hit the targets set for them.

Competency is the skill which allows your team members to do their job. If a team member is incompetent, team performance can be jeopardized. When a team member is weak in an area, once again, TRAIN THEM! Give them the training and knowledge to be successful. When you train your team, you are investing in the future of your team which in turn provides you a very good return on your investment (ROI). Sir Richard Branson said: "Train people well so they can leave, treat them well enough so they don't want to."

By training and treating your people well, builds the team you want. It allows you to balance the team's workload when it comes to delivering your product or project to your customer. With a well-trained workforce you are no longer dependent on a select few team members and can depend on the whole team.

Have a good lesson plan in place and set-up your team members to where they are fundamentally well trained in what they are responsible and accountable for delivering within your team. Use the people on your team that have the creative talent to teach, the experience to teach and they have a good understanding in your team techniques, your team process, to TRAIN others on your team and even outside of your team, when it is required. Set-up lunch box training sessions for your team and use the ones that have the talent and experience to teach the ones that are less talented and experienced. Your lesson plan is just like your team process. It is a living and well documented process. Pictures, drawings, diagrams and GUI screen shots detailing step-by-step process functions has always been part of a good lesson plan when you create one. Good fundamental techniques:

- Are tied back to your team process and what your team is empowered to do through RAA.
- Lead to great results.
- Are the "right way" for doing things and are part of the SO in your SWOT Analysis.
- Deal with threats to your team.

As an example, in a baseball game, when the bases are loaded with no outs, the infield will play in and the pitcher will pitch around the hitter trying to force a grounder so that his infield teammates can field the ball and throw out the runner on third base as he approaches home plate. This fundamental technique is something your team has learned from a coach who has the experience to deal with these types of situations and your team has practiced this technique so that they can successfully get the runner out at home plate. By learning the correct techniques, your team will know how to handle and deal with adversity. Bad techniques:

- Lead to team inconsistency, ambiguity and uncertainty through a poorly defined team process.
- Teach your team the "wrong way" for doing things.

Don't act like a bunch of monkeys where your team gets caught up in a "We have always done it this way" type of situation or culture from what bad techniques can bring to your team.

The "WT" of SWOT

Bad techniques are identified and represent the WT (weakness or threat) in your SWOT analysis. A weakness or a threat can:

- Impact the overall "safety" of your team.
- Take people out of their comfort zone.
- Can go against your team's shared cultural norms.

An easy way to remember a weakness or a threat and how to react to it is "WhaT's the MATA." In addressing a Weakness or a Threat, WT, you will Mitigate, Accept, Transfer or Avoid it (MATA) within your SWOT analysis. In a team situation, the best approach to take when it comes to dealing with "WT" is to mitigate your response. Use the problem-solving techniques presented earlier in this book to help you in the mitigation. Bad techniques, weaknesses and threats represent everything you don't want with your team and are the areas for improvement. With every team, there is room for improvement and properly handling bad techniques, weaknesses and threats are where improvements can be made.

Tying it together, People and TET

Tying it together, the third part of your foundation's building block, TET. A well-defined, fundamentally sound, consistent and repeatable team process provides you great results.

- Through your team process, you have taught your team the "right way" for getting things done.
- They are gaining the "right" experience from the right environment through your team process.
- With your team process in place, your team will know how to handle adversity.
- It gives your team the "right" fundamental direction they need to be successful which can be inspiring.

A great example for how TET can inspire your people comes from former Head Coach Bill Walsh of the San Francisco 49'ers. When Coach Walsh joined the 49'ers, he brought with him his West Coast Offense and through his own talents, experience and techniques (TET) was able to create a football dynasty that inspired his team to win 3 Super Bowls. As Bill Walsh said: "There are winners, and there are people who would like to be winners but just don't know how to do it. Intelligent and talented people who are motivated can learn how to become winners if they have someone who will teach them."

Now back to the team process. When the team process is ill conceived or poorly defined, you are teaching your team the "wrong way" of doing things. They gain the "wrong" experience in the wrong environment and if they move on later in their career to a new team, they will take with them these "wrong" techniques, which if not kept in check, will spread like a virus through your institution (or other institutions) leading to missed opportunities and poor results. DO NOT LET THIS HAPPEN! You as a leader are responsible for keeping this from happening ensuring that good fundamental techniques are in place and the "right" experience is learned and gained by your team.

When it comes to tying together the attributes of your team, you must know your team.

- Know your team and be a leader.
- Where team members need training, get it for them.

- Set-up a mentorship program within your team where your talented and experienced team members coach and train your less talented and experienced team members.

Agile Manifesto and the Scrum Guide – A Business Application

The Agile Manifesto and the term "Agile" continue to gain a lot of popularity as a project management or product delivery process. Within the Agile Manifesto, pairing, grouping or co-location amongst team members is a key process attribute that is followed. This grouping can be done within your team to help your less talented and experienced team members learn and gain experience from your more talented and experienced team members. As time progresses and your team gains more experience and gets better at their jobs, they become a more balanced and cohesive team, a key goal for Agile-based teams. As it relates to this book are listed four key principles from the Twelve Principles of the Agile Manifesto. These four Agile Manifesto principles are:

- Business people and developers must work together daily throughout the project.
- Build projects around motivated individuals. Give them the environment and support they need and trust them to get the job done.
- The best architectures, requirements and designs emerge from self-organizing teams.
- At regular intervals, the team reflects on how to become more effective, then tunes and adjusts its behavior accordingly.

A prime example of an Agile company is Facebook. Once again from the book *Talent Wins*, they state that: "Agile companies like Facebook have "a fixed backbone" of structure, processes and governance to support "looser" more dynamic elements that can be adapted quickly to new challenges and opportunities. These companies create signature processes to differentiate them from the competition, but they do not prescribe the details for how their teams get the work done. They empower their teams to come up with creative solutions to the rapidly evolving challenges they face." RAA, PAA, TET; The Power to Motivate People can provide you the tools, techniques and guidelines when creating the solutions needed for creating your own signature process and for empowering your team.

As teams became more accustomed to following the Agile Manifesto, this led to the development of the Scrum Guide. Within the Scrum Guide, the team members would become part of a Scrum Team which includes a Product Owner, a Scrum Master and the Development Team. To work effectively within the Scrum Team, everyone on the team would:

- Follow a common goal.
- Follow and adhere to the same cultural norms.
- Respect and trust one another when it came time to delivering a quality product and as the Scrum Guide would refer to it, "a functional" product to your customer.

Now back to the grouping of your team members. Where pairing, grouping or co-location of your team members is not possible, make sure open communication channels exist. To assist you in this area, you can build virtual PODS where your remote teams can come together on a consistent and regular basis to communicate, coordinate, cooperate and collaborate on key team activities. Use modern technology like cellular telephones, Instant Messenger, video conferencing, e-mail and finally in some cases, social media to interact and communicate amongst your team, with your external partners and your customer.

Use lunch-box training sessions for training your team members. Many successful institutions use lunch-box training sessions on a regular basis. As an example, various teams within these institutions would set up their training sessions in their cafeteria to conduct this training. They would send an invite to everyone at the institutional facility and attendance was always considered optional. It was a great way of integrating across the institution and getting the word out as to the value your team brings to the institution. Doing it in the cafeteria, during lunch was a great place to conduct this training, where people could get their lunch, sit, relax and learn.

Expanded People and TET Table Summary

Building your team	• Power, Motivation and People along with taking the initiative
• People	• Know your team, operate as a team • Collaborate, share the common goal • Tie back to your repeatable team process • Practice the good "C" words • Be in control and take charge by taking ownership
• Talent	• Be creative • EASE. Enhance, accept, share and exploit team talents • Empowerment and freedom
• Experience	• Be an active participant • Know that it is a coordinated effort • Set up the right working environment and experience where it is fundamentally sound, consistent and repeatable
• Technique	• Aim your team in the right direction with the right fundamental process • Take control and lead your team • Lead by example, set the example • Continually offer the best training • Remove bad techniques from your team process • Know the difference between the right way and the wrong way of doing things • Create the right fundamental team environment • Make improvements, when they are required

Self-directed People and TET

Most of the information in this section provides you the tools and techniques to help you lead. But what can it directly do for you? The answer is simple. It:

- Can make you a better leader.
- Gives you the fundamental tools, principles and techniques to lead an effective team.
- Shows others that you understand what it takes to lead a team through a well thought-out fundamental team process.

- Shows that you understand what it takes to be an effective leader because you mapped out your team's process and set the direction you want your team to follow.

Now when you look back at the team process along with the tools and principles you have put it place, what can you do to make you a better individual, a better team member, a better leader? Once again, the answer can be simple. Be aware of your own creative talents and what your own strengths and weaknesses are. John C. Maxwell said: "Good leadership begins with leaders knowing who they are. They know their own strengths and weaknesses. They know that self-knowledge is foundational to effective leadership." Run your own SWOT analysis against your own strengths and weaknesses and from there, look for areas of self-improvement. There is always room for improvement even in areas you are good at.

In Ken Burn's 1st episode of *The Civil War*, President Abraham Lincoln is quoted as saying "All men have the right to rise as far as talent would take them, just as he had." Along with President Abraham Lincoln's quote above, in the movie *War Machine*, the US Ambassador to Afghanistan tells fictional General Glen McMahon: "You gotta rise as your talents dictate." And finally, from Emily Dickinson and one of her poems as stated from the movie *Seabiscuit*:

"We never know how high we are

   Till we are called to rise;

And then, if we are true to plan,

   Our statures touch the skies—"

For areas that you are good at and have the creative talent for, plan and then challenge yourself to rise up, use, exploit and enhance your talents and abilities. And when rising up to the talents you possess, do not abuse your own talents in the areas you are good at. A great example of abusing your own talents comes from the classic movie, *The Hustler*. "Fast Eddie" Felson was a billiard player talented enough to take on one of the best billiard players in the world at the time, Minnesota Fats. In the opening scene, Fast Eddie challenges Minnesota Fats to a billiards game only to lose to Minnesota Fats badly at the start of the movie. In their first meeting, Fast Eddie had the creative talent to win, but did not have the experience and character to win at Minnesota Fats' level. It was later on in the movie that Fast Eddie learned what it took to win at that level, which involved character. In Fast Eddie's second match with Minnesota Fats, Fast Eddie let everyone know that "It is not enough that you just have talent, you have to have character too." Share your creative talents with others in a positive way. People can learn from them.

- BE A POSITIVE ROLE MODEL.
- BE A MENTOR.
- BE A COACH.

For items that you are weak in, once again look for improvement. Search for and then attend seminars on subject areas you want to improve. Take control, educate and train yourself. General Wesley Clark said: "I've never met an effective leader who wasn't aware of his talents and working to sharpen them." Take aim and hit the targets which you set for yourself and the targets set by your team leaders. Continually look for new information that can better improve yourself and your team. Be a lifelong learner and never stop learning. Henry Ford said: "Anyone who stops learning is old, whether at twenty or eighty. Anyone who keeps learning stays young." Always be a student where learning something new makes you a better person, a better leader. Always look for new tools and techniques that you can apply to all the situations you may run into in life. Stay confident in knowing that you can improve yourself and others around you and do so with the utmost level of integrity.

Daniel Goleman, Richard Boyatzis and Annie McKee said: "The most meaningful act of responsibility that leaders can do is to control their own state of mind." Stay level-headed, stay humble and don't let your emotions or ego run amok, especially when it comes to leading a team or communicating ways that can improve a team. In the movie, _The Godfather_, one of the best lines was "It's just business." Don't take business criticism as a personal attack because for the most part it is not. Accept constructive criticism as it relates to your team process and improve in the areas that require improvement.

Always stay flexible to changing circumstances and deal with the change when they appear. The business world is continually evolving and changing. Change with it. Keep up with the change or be left out when it does come and leaves you behind. As a leader, lead and make the change. Be in control, take charge and take ownership. Always stay positive in the knowledge that the things you introduce to others can bring value to them and look to them to apply this value to their own personal and business lives and to their own personal and business leadership situations.

Applying the "I" – Taking the initiative

Building your team	• Power, Motivation and People along with taking the initiative
• "I"	• Taking the initiative • Applying the *"I's"*

("I") – The final part of the lead acronym, *PMPI* is very important. It represents:

- Taking the INITIATIVE and building your team through RAA, PAA, TET.
- Applying the *"I's"* when it comes to your team.

Going back to Jeffrey Gitomer, we learn his 1st Principle for Selling which is "Kick your own Ass." This applies to YOU taking the initiative when building your team through RAA, PAA, TET and applying the tools provided to you in this book. Take the initiative and put in motion the steps for making your team better at what they do. Stephen Covey's Habit 1: "Be Proactive", went even further than just "Taking the Initiative." "Being Proactive was more than just "Taking the Initiative." It meant we were responsible and that our behavior was a function of our decisions, and not our conditions. We have the initiative and the responsibility to make things happen from which proactive people are driven by values – carefully thought about, selected and internalized values." RAA, PAA, TET can provide you those values.

- BE PROACTIVE.
- BE RESPONSIBLE.
- BE A LEADER.
- BE IN CONTROL, TAKE CHARGE AND TAKE OWNERSHIP.

Don't get caught in the monkey rut of "We have always done it this way." "Kick your own Ass" to getting it done. INVEST in your people. Invest your resources, time and efforts in developing your team.

A team process created but not IMPLEMENTED does nothing for you. It brings no value and can make your team feel like "What's the point." "We put this wonderful team process in place, but no one is using it." This is where you, as a leader now leads. Take the proper steps for INTRODUCING and implementing the building of your team and putting into motion the RAA, PAA, TET principles into your team process. Do so with the utmost level of INTEGRITY. INSPIRE others to embrace the RAA, PAA, TET principles. Gain buy-in from them after you implement the principles for your own team and then communicate to everyone that has an interest in your team process that it is ready for use by your team. Inspire others into building their own teams through RAA, PAA, TET. INTEGRATE the RAA, PAA, TET principles into your institution's mainstream. INCLUDE everyone.

Steve Jobs said: "Innovation distinguishes between a leader and a follower." Be INNOVATIVE when creating your team process. Plan and prepare for your team's future through this innovation. Be innovative with some level of INGENUITY when you introduce your team process and the RAA, PAA, TET principles to others. Allow your team to bring with them their own level of ingenuity. As an example, General Patton said: "Never tell people how to do things, tell them what to do and they will surprise you with their ingenuity." Albert Einstein said: "Imagination is more important than knowledge." Muhammed Ali said: "A man who has no imagination has no wings." Use your IMAGINATION when it comes to you developing your team process. Be an imaginative, critical and creative thinker when developing your team process and allow your team to do the same when it comes to them executing your process.

As stated before, Steve Jobs said: "Have the courage to follow your heart and intuition. They somehow already know what you truly want to become. Everything else is secondary." Follow your heart and what you believe in when it comes to the process you have put in place. Create a little fanfare showing everyone the importance to having a well-documented team process and the value it brings to your team. Inspire and INFLUENCE your team through your positive actions. Lead by example. Set the example.

INSPECT and track how well your team process is working based on the value-added quality controls you put in place and always look for areas of IMPROVEMENT based on its results, then make the change where change is required. The changes can be small incremental changes or ITERATIONS, to major improvements. When you do make a change, make sure you communicate the change so that everyone knows and understand the impacts the change will have to their own teams, your internal and external partners and your customer.

Maintain a positive relationship with your external partners and your customer. INTERACT with them on a continual basis. Where you can, INVITE them to institutional events. Invite them out in an informal setting where they can relax and just be themselves. Informal meet and greets at sporting events like a soccer game, a football game or a baseball game come to mind. By staying relaxed at these meet and greets, your external partners and your customer will be more open to discussing their likes and dislikes when it comes to your team process and the products you deliver. LISTEN to them and let them know that their INPUT is always valuable.

Because we are talking about the *I*'s and what they can mean to you and your team, let's add one that when combined with four "C's", is extremely valuable. In the US Army's Military Intelligence, there is an acronym used to describe the top Military Intelligence organization or unit. This is C4I, which represents Communication, Command, Control, Computers and INTELLIGENCE. You have already learned several other top "C's" for leading and dealing with people. When it comes to C4I, in this book, there will be a brief description of what they mean to you and your team.

- Set-up your team where there is open communication, internally and externally.
- Put in place within your team process the steps where your team can take control of all the scenarios they may encounter through empowerment.

- Provide your team the best tools available in computer technology and software and always keep your computers and software up-to-date after they go into production.
- Provide your team with the tools and the processes to help them make intelligent choices, the right decisions when it comes to your team process and your customer. Set the direction for your team to follow in order to be successful.

And finally, INVIGORATE yourself and your team. Stay active, energetic and positive. When changes to you and your team are required, understand why the change is required and RE-INVENT yourself along with your team. This is especially important when it comes to keeping up with the vast technological advancements we are experiencing today or staying ahead of your competition.

Quality Management and Kaizen – A Business Application

Now that we have progressed through the steps for building your team through RAA, PAA, TET, some process improvement initiatives may need to take place.

Improvement is an important element of everything you do. It is also important to know that performance measurements which drive improvement can be subjective in nature. Everyone has an opinion on what needs to be measured and how it should be measured. Make sure you are very clear with your team on the performance measurements you put in place and gain their buy-in when implementing your performance measurements or metrics. You will look for areas of improvement starting with your initial planning all the way down to any operational process improvement initiatives you will want to take on and conduct to make your team and how they operate better. Six Sigma and Kaizen are some of the top-quality management areas you can use for process improvement. Kaizen:

- Is gradual unending improvement by doing the little things better along with setting and achieving increasingly higher standards.
- Events enhance process control and reduce non-value activities within the process which makes the team more productive and allows for closer process focus by all involved in the process.
- Provides a method for incremental improvement.

The benefits of Kaizen are:

- Teamwork.
- Personal discipline.
- Improved moral.
- Quality circles.
- Suggestions for improvement.

Quality Management, Six Sigma and Lean Six Sigma – A Business Application

Six Sigma and Lean Six Sigma provides you great process steps and tools through their DMAIC (Define, Measure, Analyze, Improve and Control) process areas for improving any functional or operational process you may have. As it relates to Lean Six Sigma, their first three laws are important when it comes to your team. They are the:

- 1st Lean Six Sigma Law: Law of Flexibility – Process velocity is directly proportional to the flexibility of a given process.
- 2nd Lean Six Sigma Law: Law of Focus – 20% of activities cause 80% of delays in a given process.
- 3rd Lean Six Sigma Law: Law of Velocity – The velocity of any process is inversely proportional to the amount of WIP (Work in progress).

Stay flexible when dealing with your team, your internal and external partners and your customer. Stay focused on your team's mission and hitting your customer deliverables. Stay focused and maintain the velocity, the initiative for building your team through RAA, PAA, TET while also understanding the impacts the RAA, PAA, TET initiative may have to your team's current workload. The time it takes for building your team through RAA, PAA, TET is up to you and what your team can handle. Maintain a comfortable balance for building your team through RAA, PAA, TET and your team's current responsibilities or commitments, especially when it comes to your customer deliverables.

When utilizing systematic quality activities and setting up a quality management organization, following the CMMI Process Areas and then advancing up the CMMI Capability or Maturity Levels can be beneficial to you and your team if you decide to use CMMI as a framework for your team process.

Benjamin Franklin said: "An ounce of prevention is worth a pound of cure." It is your job to ensure everyone on your team knows what they are entrusted to do within your team process and that you have a process in place that works. In the areas of improvement, there are many quality management tools at your disposal. They are used to help you improve an existing process, map out a new process, solve problems and provide the decision makers the tools and information they need to come up with a solution to a problem. Some of the quality management improvement tools listed in this section are part of ASQ's Seven Management and Planning Tools and ASQ's Seven Basic Tools of Quality, which are identified when describing the quality management tool in this section of the book. Also included are other important quality tools which are easy to use and manage within your team's quality improvement initiatives. USE THEM! They can help you improve. They can bring value.

The American Society for Quality (ASQ) – A Business Application

The American Society for Quality (ASQ) is a good place to research some really good quality management reference material. Within this context, this book provides you the quality management improvement tools that are easy to understand and implement. They are:

- Brainstorming.
- Affinity Diagram.
- Nominal Group Technique.
- Inter-relational Digraph.
- Flowcharting (functional or transactional process-related; or cross-functional process-related, swim lanes).
- Data Collection and GAP Analysis.
- Root Cause Analysis (RCA) which includes:
  o Fault Tree Diagram and The 5 Whys (as additional support to the Cause-and-Effect Diagram and the Pareto Chart).
  o Cause-and-Effect Diagram, Isakawa Diagram or Fishbone Diagram.
  o Pareto Chart.
- Control Chart.
- Dashboards and Benchmarking.

Examples and templates of these tools can be found in Appendix A.

Brainstorming

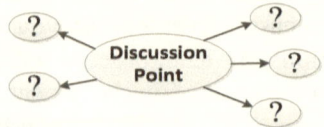

When it comes to brainstorming, Linus Paulding said: "The best way to get a good idea is to get lots of ideas." Brainstorming is good for gathering a lot of ideas to include your initial team's definition. Through it, you will identify the subject matter you want to cover. You will then record all the ideas within a set timeframe. All ideas are accepted without criticism and everyone is expected to participate. This will go on until all ideas are recorded or you run out of time.

Affinity Diagram (ASQ Seven Management and Planning Tools)

From your brainstorming session your team will then take the list of ideas and organize them into groups, categories or buckets. You will then have your team remove any duplicates where needed.

Nominal Group Technique

Idea	Name 1 / Value	Name 2 / Value	Name 3 / Value	Total	Rank
Idea 1	1	2	1	4	1
Idea 2	3	3	2	8	3
Idea 3	2	1	3	6	2
Idea 4	4	4	4	12	4

Through nominal group technique, you will take your list of ideas as they relate to the subject matter and have each team member prioritize or rank them, 1 to 5 as an example. The initial ranking will be done on the individual level, which will then be followed at the group level. When complete, you will then record them to get a weighted score based on each team member's ranking.

Inter-relational Digraph (ASQ Seven Management and Planning Tools)

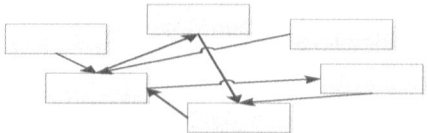

Inter-relational digraph is used similar to an affinity diagram with the exception is that it provides you a list of ideas as they relate to your subject matter. The list of ideas are identified and placed on a board in no particular order. Once all the ideas are identified, you will determine which ideas influence the other ideas and you will begin to draw arrows from the least influential idea to next higher influential idea. This can be done in any order, but using a circular pattern (or clockwise motion, as an example) for doing your analysis is the most effective. You do this comparison or inter-relational analysis until all ideas are either related or non-related. Once again, brainstorming techniques are extremely effective in this exercise.

Flowcharting (ASQ Seven Basic Tools of Quality)

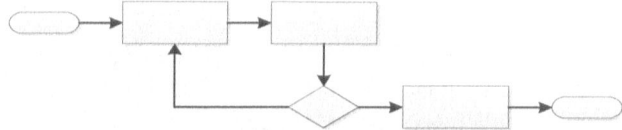

Flowcharting (process (functional or transactional) or cross-functional (swim lanes)) is used to map out your team process. It is used when you first form your team for mapping out a new process to when you want to make process improvements to an existing process. It is a living documented process that if done properly and communicated effectively can deliver optimal results. You can brainstorm your list of ideas and their relationships to each other prior to conducting your flowcharting exercise.

Data Collection and GAP Analysis

Data collection and GAP analysis is process analysis. It is used to measure your current process. From there you will run a GAP analysis to compare your current "AS-IS" process to a "TO-BE" desired process where improvements can be made where they may be required. This can be especially important as change occurs on a regular basis. This can be done at the business, process or product level. From your data collection you can also create control charts, run charts and scatter diagrams based on the data. These charts and diagrams are also parts of the Seven Tools of Quality Management.

Root Cause Analysis (RCA)

Root cause analysis (RCA) is used to find the root cause of problem defects and eliminating the defects that don't apply. RCA tools include:

- Fault Tree Diagrams.
- The 5 Whys.
- Cause and Effect Diagrams.
- Pareto Charts.

Fault Tree Diagram

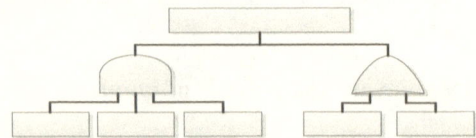

The fault tree diagram is used to take the problem statement and drill down to the actual root cause of the problem. It is extremely effective when used with The 5 Whys question and answer session.

The 5 Whys

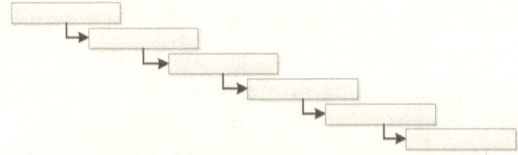

The 5 Whys is a technique that begins by asking why the initial problem occurred and based on the answer drilling down up to 5 levels to get to the true root cause or defect. In addition to being used with the fault tree

diagram, the 5 Whys are also used with all of the other RCA tools and templates which are provided in Appendix A. "The 5 Whys" type question and answer session when combined with SMART and EEI is also extremely beneficial and effective when defining your team process and your team's responsibilities. What your team is empowered to do, what they are accountable for and the authority levels they may have in the decision-making process.

Cause and Effect Diagram (ASQ Seven Basic Tools of Quality)

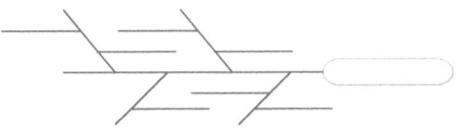

Cause and effect diagram - also referred to as the Isakawa diagram or the fishbone diagram. This diagram uses the 7M categories as defined by the ASQ as they relate to your problem. The problem is identified via a problem statement. It was originally considered the 6Ms before Mother Nature was added. The 7M categories are Mother Nature, Materials, Methods, Manpower, Measurement, Machines and Management. The 7Ms provide you the basis for identifying your defect as it relates to its "M" category and your problem statement. Under each M category, are sub-categories or defects that would go directly under the "M" as they relate to your problem. A brainstorming session can be used to identify additional sub-categories that may apply to your problem or to eliminate sub-categories that don't apply.

Pareto Chart (ASQ Seven Basic Tools of Quality)

Pareto charting is grouping and counting the number of defects as they relate to your overall problem. Pareto charts are used for identifying areas of variation needing improvement. You will want to reduce the amount of variation as it relates to your overall problem. The defects you identified will go on a chart to identify the top ones. Pareto charts are also used in conjunction with the 80 / 20 rule, where 80% of your problems can be solved working on the top 20% of the defects. Working on the top 3 problem areas or defects as defined in your pareto chart can also be a very effective use of your time when the 80 / 20 rule may not apply.

Control Chart (ASQ Seven Basic Tools of Quality)

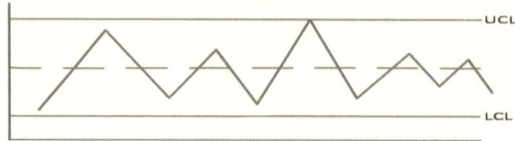

Control chart is used to measure the amount of variation or variables within a process and is excellent for measuring how well a process is performing over time along with its stability. The amount of variation in the process determines the type of corrective action or the course of action you will take when addressing the variation. The control chart will have a median line along with upper and lower control limits to help you to determine if your process is "out-of-sync" to your team's process SLA or the SLA's you provide to your customer.

Dashboards and Benchmarking

Dashboards help you track metrics associated with the accomplishment of business and / or team goals and can improve team accountability. Dashboards are also used for quick status updates and to track delivery performance. Use dashboards to minimize the need for long or "lengthy" status meetings. Using dashboards allows you to concentrate on process improvement areas when your team actually does meet, which can improve your team's efficiency and can make them better at what they do.

Dashboards can be combined with benchmarking. Benchmarking is used for measuring your performance against others that are good performers or best-in-class teams, organizations or institutions. You can benchmark strategic, operations, process and / or procedural areas. When you are looking at benchmarking, Dr. Bies said: "Move from "Yes, but", passive aggressive way of thinking to "Yes, and" way of thinking where you can build on something of value." From these performance measurements, there will be some areas that you can identify needing improvement. Once you determine there is a need for improvement, following the Six

Sigma Book of Knowledge (SSBOK) and their DMAIC (Define, Measure, Analyze, Improve and Control) process will help you develop your process improvement plan.

As you measure and improve your team process, there will be lessons to be learned. Make sure that the lessons learned are well documented and stored so that they can be used as a historical reference when they are needed later on within your process life cycle. Make sure you include the positive lessons learned along with the negative lessons learned.

These are some of the quality management improvement tools that are extremely effective. There are others that are available for use and can be found on-line just by searching for them. The ASQ web site is a great place to find and research quality management improvement tools.

Finally, bringing it all together

Now that you have your plan of attack for delivering a quality product through proper planning. Now that you defined your team's functions and mapped out your team process. Now that you have introduced RAA, PAA, TET; The Power to Motivate People into your institution's mainstream and have "Built your team" through RAA, PAA, TET. Think about this. Building a team through RAA, PAA, TET has been around for a very long time. When you look back through history you can find plenty of examples. One example is when King Leonidas of Sparta took on Xerxes of Persia at the Battle of Thermopylae. The Persians greatly outnumbered King Leonidas and his men, but yet they were able to hold off the Persians for more than a week. Why were they able to do this? The answer is simple. King Leonidas gave his men the fundamental tools and techniques to be successful through principles similar to RAA, PAA, TET. King Leonidas:

- Took control and was in charge of the situation they faced.
- Led by example and set the example for his men to follow.
- Instilled the confidence in his men to follow through his leadership, his loyalty and his actions. His men were ready to take on any challenge even when the odds were greatly against them.

Your team can be no different when you "Build your team" through RAA, PAA, TET. When you bring it all together, building your team through RAA, PAA, TET, you have taken the steps where:

- Your team can take ownership of their jobs and their decision-making.
- Your team can take control and be in charge.
- You have instilled the confidence a team needs to be successful.
- Your team is empowered and can accomplish any job or task that is presented to them.
- They are trusted, respected and reliable.

- They have been taught how to perform and lead.
- Through you empowering them, they are gaining the "right" experience from the right cultural environment.
- There is a sense of belonging amongst them within the shared community you have created for them.
- They believe in what they do and their work means something to them.
- You have put in place the tools and techniques within in your team process to minimize the need for fire drills and crisis modes, especially when it comes to your customer's deliverables.
- You have put in place the tools and techniques within your team process to make improvements, when improvements need to be made.
- Your team has the ability to run a SWOT analysis when it is needed and they have the ability to react and respond to it based on its results.

Not only is your team empowered for success; you, yourself, are empowered to making your team even better as time progresses, technology changes and business requirements change. And when the change does occur you will be ready for it. One of the main intentions of this book is to provide you a fundamental framework you can build your team on. Based on this, take and only use the building your team through RAA, PAA, TET principles that currently fit your team's environment and implement them based on your team's current needs. Run a pilot program and implement the RAA, PAA, TET principles your team is comfortable with first to get a quick win. This can allow you to build up your team's confidence when it comes to you implementing the remaining RAA, PAA, TET principles once your team is ready for them later on.

And to finally close out things. There are hundreds of outstanding books on team and motivational leadership. This book is no different than theirs except for one simple thing. Building your team through RAA, PAA, TET is like a cheer. It is easy to say and remember. And with it easy to remember, through RAA, PAA, TET you will have the Power to Motivate your People and through this Power, you will have the Playbook for Your Success. It is easy to remember, something that once you and your team get used to it, you and your team will never forget.

An added Bonus, COIL

COIL	• Be Creative • Communicate, Collaborate and Control the Essentials, the Fundamentals • Operate and Optimize • Initiate, Integrate and Improve (7 Management and Planning Tools, 7 Basic Tools of Quality Management) • LEAD, Listen and Learn

There have been a lot of acronyms introduced to you to learn and apply. Provided below is one more as an added bonus. This leadership bonus acronym is COIL. COIL represents:

- C – Be Creative; Communicate, Collaborate and Control.
- O – Operate and Optimize.
- I – Initiate, Integrate and Improve.
- L – LEAD, Listen and Learn.

By following COIL, you will prevent RECOIL. RECOIL can happen, when a process is not well defined or not followed, when fundamental team principles are not applied. It can lead to inactivity within your team along with delivering a poor-quality product to your customer. A product you will most likely have to do over. Inactivity because of RECOIL leads to inconsistency, ambiguity and uncertainty within your team. If you have "flow-through" in your team process, the product you are producing for your customer should "flow-through" your system with very few problems or defects. COIL can provide you that "flow-through" in your team process.

There is a general law of Physics where "Every action has an equal and opposite reaction." While this may work well in the "Physics world", it may not go over well in the "Business World." Let's explain.

In Physics, if you punch a wall and you are unable to put your fist through the wall, the amount of force you are applying or putting forward will come back at you with an equal and opposite amount of force from which it was applied. This can lead to you breaking your hand because this REAL, equal and opposite force will have as much power and force from which you put forth when you decided to slam your fist into the wall. Now if you are able to break through the wall, great, some of this equal and opposite force will dissipate as the force from the wall will be dispersed into space through the opening you just left, the breaking and opening of the wall.

In the "Business World", when you face a barrier, break through it. Reduce the amount of RECOIL you will experience. Don't sit back and expect things to happen on their own because usually, they don't. With no action, how can you expect a reaction, positive or negative. Use COIL and the RAA, PAA, TET principles to force the positive reaction.

C – Be Creative; Communicate, Collaborate and Control

Through this new leadership acronym, COIL. You will:

- Be creative and you will allow creativity to be integral part of your team process.
- Communicate, collaborate and control the essentials, the fundamentals RAA, PAA, TET can bring to you and your team.
- Maintain open communication to ensure the flow of information takes place and that your project or product deliverables can be met.
- Maintain open communication with your team for communicating the essentials, your team fundamentals.
- BE A LEADER. Take control of your team and your team process and then take the necessary action to force a positive reaction when it comes to leading your team.
- Collaborate within your team when defining the necessary action that will force this positive reaction and through your team collaboration,

allow your team to take control and ownership of the things they own within your team process.
- Put controls in place via KPIs and SLAs for your team process.
- Stay committed to your mission and deliver to your customer a high-quality product.
- Communicate your level of commitment to everyone that has an interest in your team process.

It is also important to note, with COIL, you can expand and include as many of the good "C" words as you wish which are covered in the People section of this book.

O – Operate and Optimize

You will:

- Optimize your current operations.
- Empower and then entrust within your team, their ability to perform their job at the highest level they are capable of performing to ensure that team optimization is in place for your team.
- Have effective processes in place and always make process improvements within your operation.

I – Initiate, Integrate and Improve

You will:

- Take the initiative and integrate across your institution and to your external partners your team process.
- Explain to them what a well-defined team process can bring to them with your open communication.
- Continually improve your process.
- Develop a process improvement plan for the improvement areas you identify and then take the proper action for putting the process improvement plan in place for making your team better at what they do.

L – LEAD, Listen and Learn

President John F. Kennedy said: "Leadership and learning are indispensable to each other." Through this, you will:

- LEAD BY EXAMPLE. SET THE EXAMPLE.
- BE A LEADER for your team.
- Be aware of your surroundings.
- OPEN YOUR MIND, YOUR EYES AND YOUR EARS.
- Listen to your team and your customers. Be an active listener. Their feedback to your communications is essential for improvement.

I am sure you have noticed already; this book pulls some amazing quotes and phrases from different media streams. By actively listening (and reading), we have applied to this book key quotes and phrases that bring value to your team and to your customer that are representative of the RAA, PAA, TET principles.

Now, going back to Coach Tom Izzo, he stressed the importance of being an active listener. He always looked for new basketball recruits that had the ability to "Learn to listen, Listen to learn." When it comes to your team and your customer, everyone's input or feedback is important therefore you and your team should be no different. Listen to what your:

- Customer is telling you and if improvements are required, make the change.
- Team has to say, good or bad and make the change for the betterment of the team and your customer.

And finally, you will learn from your process results along with the timelines for delivering a high-quality product to your customer and you will make the necessary process improvement changes based on the results you receive.

"So how do you get there?" Be fearless. In rock climbing there is an old saying: "When in doubt, muscle out." When are you are not sure of your next step or handhold or not sure of the direction you need to climb it is better to go than to freeze and just sit there letting your muscles tire out "sitting there" thinking about it. Sometimes going with your gut is better than just sitting there being idle. If it works, great! Document what you did right and add it to your "living" documented team process. If it did not work as well as you had planned then make the proper adjustments and continue moving forward. "Where is all of this going?" It is simple. When leading your team:

- COIL to avoid RECOIL.
- COIL to deliver a timely quality product to your customer. A high-quality product that does not require re-work.
- Give your team the confidence they need to be successful, where they won't freeze or tense up questioning every little move they make.
- Have a well-defined team process in place that keeps your team members from questioning who does what, what we need to do, where we need to do it, when we need to do it, why we need to do it and how we do it.
- And finally, apply the building your team through RAA, PAA, TET principles.

Through TI VUM, building your team through RAA, PAA, TET and COIL you and your team can be successful.

Reference Summary Table

Building your Team through RAA, PAA, TET Summary Table		
TI VUM	• Take the Initiative • Have a Vision • Basic to Thorough Understanding of the Essentials, the Fundamentals • Move and Motivate (Move on IT)	
Planning	• Taking the Initiative, Planning, Executing, Tracking Progress, Finalizing and Approving	
Team Dynamics	• Be SMART in your approach – Specific, Measurable, Attainable, Realistic and Timely • Forming, Storming, Norming and Performing; setting up the right fundamental team environment and culture. One of value	
Process Dynamics	• The Essential Elements of Information (EEI) of Who, What, Where, When, How and Why	
Process Mapping and Process Narrative	• Avoid the "5 Monkeys" • Team Mission Statement • Team Charter • Overall Team Process, Process Map and Workflow	
The Contract	• Your contract and your Team Member's Contract	
Building your team	• **Power, Motivation and People along with taking the initiative**	
• Power	• Responsibility – Defined Roles and Responsibilities, RACI Model and Job Guidelines with meaning and direction • Accountability – Defined areas of Accountability, Ownership and Decision Making • Authority – Defined Authority levels and Decision Making	
• Motivation	• Power – Empowerment through mutual respect and trust • Achievement – Through accomplishment, through recognition and reward • Affiliation – A sense of belonging, a sense of community	
• People	• Talent – Knowing Strengths, Weaknesses, Opportunities and Threats through SWOT Analysis, "SO EASE into it…." • Experience – The "right" experience vs. the "wrong" experience • Technique – Process, SWOT Analysis, "WhaT's the MATA…."	
• *"I"*	• Taking the initiative • Applying the *"I's"*	
COIL	• Be Creative • Communicate, Collaborate and Control the Essentials, the Fundamentals • Operate and Optimize • Initiate, Integrate and Improve (7 Management and Planning Tools, 7 Basic Tools of Quality Management) • LEAD, Listen and Learn	

Graphical Summary

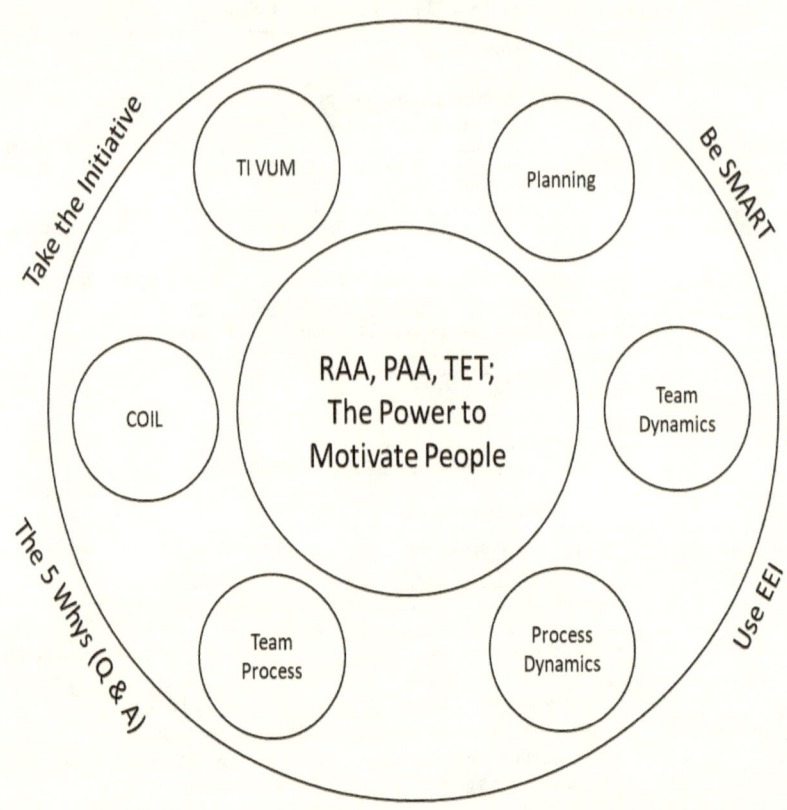

Gray Hairs and Closure

Always keep this in mind. Take the Initiative to never stop:

- Doing what you know is right for your team or your customer.
- Learning from those that came before you. There is a lot of experience behind what you can learn from the ones that came before you.

Included in Charles' journals are things he has learned from others that have come before him. These are people he worked with a long time ago which are called "Gray Hairs." If Charles hadn't started keeping his journals many years ago he never would have been able to write this book with the help from Craig.

Charles was in his 30's and working at a start-up company when he started his first journal. At the company there were a lot of young smart MBA graduates working for the company. Senior management brought in an older Consultant once with the experience to help out the start-up team in an area they were struggling with. While Charles knew the Consultant liked working with these young smart people along with their enthusiasm, you could tell the Consultant felt the company also needed some real-life experience to help the company move forward. This real-life experience would need to come from people the Consultant called "Gray Hairs." The Consultant was right. The start-up was a very good company but they did not survive the dot.com bust in the early 2000's. Gray Hairs, the basic fundamentals they have learned over the years along with the real-life experiences that they bring could have helped the teams at the start-up company.

Trusted Advisor

An excellent way of looking at this and the benefits Gray Hairs can bring comes from the movie trilogy *Lord of the Rings*. The top leader for the Fellowship of the Nine was Gandalf, the Gray. Now some of you will say, "Wait, Aragon was the returning king, therefore, he was the top leader." Aragon was the king and even kings have their trusted advisors.

That trusted advisor would be Gandalf, the Gray. Gandalf was the one all of them looked up to for advice and guidance in order to beat the Dark One. Gandalf was a Gray Hair with a vast amount of knowledge and real-life experience. Gray Hairs are the ones that influenced Charles the most in pulling together the valuable information in his journals.

Both Charles and Craig are Gray Hairs now and knowing the things they have learned from those who came before them, they are now able to share this valuable information with you. Twenty years ago, they would not have been able to bring RAA, PAA, TET; The Power to Motivate People to you. As stated before, "Best efforts without guidance lead to failure." "Technique teaches us the process for doing things and how we accomplish key tasks; while experience teaches us how to apply what we learned and how to motivate people to successfully achieve those tasks." Gray Hairs provide the guidance to help you return to the basic fundamentals and valuable real-life experience is what Gray Hairs bring to you and your team. Make sure you learn everything you can from the Gray Hairs.

And finally, to close things out in the book when it comes to your team, one key component to any team is team unity. RAA, PAA, TET; The Power to Motivate People can provide you the key components for team unity.

Appendix A – Templates and Examples

Appendix A provides you valuable templates you can use when you start your initiative for building your team through RAA, PAA, TET. Most of these templates apply to business applications, but they can be useful in other team environments. If you can use them in your team environment, use them. They can help you improve. As mentioned before, the main purpose of this book is for you and your team to follow the RAA, PAA, TET principles for building your team. If you have your own team building templates that you prefer to use over the ones provided to you in this Appendix, please feel free to do so. This Appendix includes:

- Project Charter.
- Business Requirements.
- Project Plan.
- Team Mission Statement.
- Team Charter.
- Team Process.
- Process Map:
  o Cross-Functional Swim Lane.
  o Functional or Transactional.
- The Contract.
- RACI Model.
- Job Guidelines.
- Task List.
- Process Improvement Plan (Problem Statement or Charter).
- Brainstorming.
- Affinity Diagram.
- Nominal Group Technique.
- Inter-relational Digraph.
- Data Collection and GAP Analysis.
- Root Cause Analysis (RCA):
  o Fault Tree Diagram and The 5 Whys.

- o Cause and Effect Diagram, Isakawa Diagram, or Fishbone Diagram (7Ms).
- o Pareto Chart.
- Control Chart.
- Dashboard and Benchmarking.

Project Charter

This table represents a simplified project charter that can be used when you start the building of your team. In the project charter are the business requirements, goal statement, in-scope and out-of-scope requirements, key deliverables, high-level project plan dates and your project team stakeholders.

PROJECT CHARTER	BUSINESS REQUIREMENTS
What is the project charter? • Project Title • Create the Project Charter using EEI, SMART and The 5 Whys techniques	Why is the project needed? • Business requirements and objectives
GOAL STATEMENT	**TEAM SCOPE AND DELIVERABLES**
Define the project goal *"To deliver a quality product to the customer meeting their expectations while staying within the allotted schedule and budget"*	Define what is in-scope and out-of-scope when it comes to your customer and your stakeholders • In-scope requirements • Out-of-scope requirements • Key Deliverables and Ancillary Plans (e.g. Communication Plan)
PROJECT PLAN DATES	**TEAM HIERACHY**
Project: Start Date to Finish Date TI Phase: Start Date to Finish Date Plan Phase: Start Date to Finish Date Execute Phase: Start Date to Finish Date Progress Phase: Start Date to Finish Date Final Phase: Start Date to Finish Date (Customer Expected completion is <Date>) Note: Phase dates can overlap and are defined by your customer and your Project Sponsor. These dates must be realistic and achievable.	Project Sponsor: <Name> Project Champion: <Name> Project Manager: <Name> Team Members or Stakeholders: <Names>

Business Requirements Document

Your business requirements primary objective is to identify what is in-scope vs. what is out-of-scope when executing your team building project plan. Here are some key bullets you can include in the business requirements document along with a brief definition for each.

- Objectives.
    o High level objectives as defined from the project charter.
- Business Requirements and Deliverables.
    o In-scope and out-of-scope requirements as it relates to a customer deliverable.
- Acceptance Criteria.
    o Customer acceptance.
- Requirement Boundaries.
    o Organizational, process and / or scope requirement boundaries.
- Constraints and Dependencies.
    o Items that can be a constraint to your project preventing your successful delivery.
    o Items that your project is dependent on for successful delivery.
- Assumptions.
    o Statements that can impact your project for the good or the bad that need to be proven true or false. Once proven true, can become a business rule for other projects that may follow. If proven false, they are removed.
- Business Rules.
    o Assumptions that have been proven to be "true".
- Initial Project Organization.
    o Project hierarchy and project team structure (RACI Model is extremely beneficial here).
- Initial Defined Risks.
    o Known and possible unknown risks and the steps the project team will take to address the risks as they appear.
- Schedule Milestones.
    o Milestones as you go from one project phase to the next.
- Initial Work Breakdown Structure (WBS).
    o A breakout or hierarchy of your project plan from project, phase, task, sub-task and / or work activity.

Business Requirements Document, (continued)

- Order of Magnitude Cost Estimate.
  - Iterative costs which are initially defined at the highest-level (initial rough order of magnitude (ROM) and as the business requirements are further defined are drilled down to the projected costs that can eventually be + / - 3%, 5% to 10% of your actual costs.
    - The + / - threshold will be defined by management and the budget which has been set for your project.
- Configuration Management Requirements.
  - Part of your deliverables to your customer. A breakdown of its components.
- Approval Requirements.
  - Who approves what and when they approve it along with their level of authority for approvals.
- Ancillary Plans.
  - E.g. communication, change, risk, quality plans, etc.
- Revision History Table.
  - Used for version control and acts as a change history log.

Project Plan

Your project plan is used for defining the order for the phases, processes or steps you will execute to accomplish the project objectives as defined by your team to include the dates for when the project task starts and when the project task finishes. Note: Some project activities below have been removed.

ID	Name	Calendar Days Duration	Start Date	Finish Date
1	Project: Pre-Sales / Sales / Sales Engineering SDM Process – Phase 1	133 days	May 10, 2017	September 19, 2017
2	Activity: Define Requirements	5 days	May 10, 2017	May 14, 2017
7	Phase: Pre-Sales SDM	11 days	May 22, 2017	June 1, 2017
8	Activity: Define Pre-Sales Process Map	5 days	May 22, 2017	May 26, 2017
9	Activity: Define Pre-Sales Process Narrative	5 days	May 27, 2017	May 31, 2017
10	Activity: Gain Pre-Sales Process Approval	1 day	June 1, 2017	June 1, 2017
11	Phase: Sales SDM	67 days	June 2, 2017	August 7, 2017
12	Activity: Define Sales Process Map	32 days	June 2, 2017	July 3, 2017
13	Activity: Define Sales Process Narrative	34 days	July 4, 2017	August 6, 2017
14	Activity: Gain Sales Process Approval	1 day	August 7, 2017	August 7, 2017
15	Phase: Sales Engineering (SE) SDM	33 days	August 8, 2017	September 9, 2017
16	Activity: Define SE Process Map	17 days	August 8, 2017	August 24, 2017
17	Activity: Define SE Process Narrative	15 days	August 25, 2017	September 8, 2017
18	Activity: Gain SE Process Approval	1 day	September 9, 2017	September 9, 2017
20	Phase: Implement Process	5 days	September 10, 2017	September 14, 2017
24	Phase: Close Project	5 days	September 15, 2017	September 19, 2017
25	Activity: Final Review	2 days	September 15, 2017	September 16, 2017
26	Activity: Administrative Closure	2 days	September 17, 2017	September 18, 2017
27	Activity: Lessons Learned	1 day	September 19, 2017	September 19, 2017
28	Activity: Release Resources	1 day	September 19, 2017	September 19, 2017
29	Activity: Close out Project	1 day	September 19, 2017	September 19, 2017

Team Mission Statement

Your team mission statement provides a summary of what you will deliver to your customer. It is the very first place you should point your customer to and is something every team member on your team should know by heart.

Here is an excellent example of a team mission statement taken from Stephen Covey and his book, *The 7 Habits of Highly Effective People: Powerful Lessons in Personal Change*: "Our mission is to empower people and organizations to significantly increase their performance capacity in order to achieve worthwhile purposes through understanding and living principle-centered leadership"

Team Charter

This table represents a simplified team charter. In it you have the team charter, the business benefits, mission or goal statement, what is in-scope and out-of-scope for your team and their key deliverables, the high-level project plan dates as it relates to team deliverables (when and where it is required) and your team member hierarchy. Note: The team charter structure is no different than that of a project charter.

TEAM CHARTER	BUSINESS BENEFITS
What is the team charter? • Create using EEI, SMART and The 5 Whys techniques	What are the business benefits? • Addresses how the team charter benefits your team, your institution and / or your customer
TEAM MISSION / GOAL STATEMENT	**TEAM SCOPE AND DELIVERABLES**
Defines the team's mission statement *"Our mission is to empower people and organizations to significantly increase their performance capacity in order to achieve worthwhile purposes through understanding and living principle-centered leadership"*	Define what is in-scope and what is out-of-scope when it comes to your customer • In-scope requirements • Out-of-scope requirements • Key Deliverables
PROJECT PLAN DATES as it relates to CUSTOMER DELIVERABLES (when and where it is required)	**TEAM HIERACHY**
Project: Start Date to Finish Date TI Phase: Start Date to Finish Date Plan Phase: Start Date to Finish Date Execute Phase: Start Date to Finish Date Progress Phase: Start Date to Finish Date Final Phase: Start Date to Finish Date (Customer Expected completion is <Date>) Note: As defined by your customer deliverables. Phase dates can overlap. These dates must be realistic and achievable.	Team VP: <Name> Team Director: <Name> Team Manager: <Name> Team Lead: <Name> Team Members: <Names>

Team Process

As stated in this book, the team process is the meat of your process. It represents everything your team will do for your customer. As always, when defining the key elements of the team process, be SMART in your approach, use EEI and the 5 Whys (drill down) question and answer format. The bullets below represent some key elements you can include, but they may not be all inclusive to your own team. Your institutional leadership and your team can determine what is appropriate to include in your own team process as it applies to your customer.

- Team Mission Statement.
  - Can be part of the team process or standalone.
- Team Charter.
  - Can be part of the team process or standalone.
- Executive Summary, Goals and / or Team Objectives.
  - Provides an executive summary or the overall goal for your team as it relates to your customer. Defines at a high-level what you plan on delivering to your customer.
- Team Leadership Hierarchy.
  - A point-of-contact (POC) list of your management team to include, but not limited to: Vice Presidents, Directors, Managers, Supervisors and / or Team Leads.
- RACI Model and Team Roles and Responsibilities.
  - Responsible, Accountable, Consulting and Informing Model of your team. In addition to the RACI Model (matrix), defined team roles and responsibilities to your customer to let your customer know who does what when it comes to the customer deliverable.
- Authority Levels.
  - Authority levels when it comes to making key decisions as they relate to your customer. Can be in written or table format.
- Team Process Map and Narrative.
  - A process map and narrative of the team process. The process narrative is used to further define a step within your process map where there may be a text-count or size limitation in its graphical representation.
- Customer Deliverables.
  - All defined in-scope customer deliverables.

Team Process, (continued)

- Customer Non-Deliverables.
  - All defined out-of-scope deliverables. Items you are not responsible for delivering to your customer.
- Customer Acceptance Criteria.
  - Acceptance criteria as defined by your customer. Can include:
    - Usability.
    - Capability.
    - Navigational.
    - Functional.
    - Security.
- Third-Party Requirements
  - All third-party requirements as it relates to in-scope deliverables to your customer.
- Team Process Constraints.
  - Constraints that may prevent successful customer in-scope delivery. Can be system or human factors related.
- Team Process Dependencies.
  - Dependencies as it relates to your customer in-scope deliverables. Can be system or human factors related.
- Team Process Assumptions.
  - Assumptions presumed to be real until proven otherwise.
- Team Process Business Rule.
  - A proven "true" team process assumption.
- Environment.
  - Environmental factors that can positively or negatively impact the Team Process. Can be:
    - Operational.
    - Organizational.
    - System related.
- Reporting Requirements.
  - All reporting requirements and their delivery frequency as it relates to your process and your customer.
- Communication Plan.
  - Communication plan for your process and your customer.

Team Process, (continued)

- Change Plan.
  - How you handle changes to your process and / or customer in-scope deliverables. Note: Out-of-scope requirements would go through change management to be approved as new in-scope deliverables.
- Risk Plan.
  - How you handle risks as they relate to your process and customer in-scope deliverables. This can include qualitative and quantitative risk analysis.
- Quality Plan.
  - Steps and processes for delivering a quality process or product.
- Signatures and Approvals.
  - Who signs what and their approval levels (can be determined by scope size and / or budget size).
- Non-Disclosure Agreements (NDA, Security).
  - All NDAs on file to protect proprietary and intellectual property information.
- Supporting Documentation.
  - Other team processes, SOPs, team playbooks and related documentation as it relates to your process and your customer (a Safety Plan as an example).
- Team Process Terms and Definitions.
  - Acronym list and their definition. A data dictionary.
- In-Scope Use Cases and Scenarios.
  - Use cases and scenarios as they relate to your process and your customer deliverables. Can include: New, MACD (Move, Add, Change, Disconnect or Delete) use cases and scenarios.
- Out-of-Scope Scenarios.
  - Items and scenarios your team will not perform or are not responsible for as it relates to a customer or a customer deliverable.
- Team Process Appendix and References.
- Revision History Table.
  - Used for version control and acts as a change history log.

Process Map – Cross-Functional Swim Lanes, or Functional or Transactional (ASQ Seven Basic Tools of Quality)

Process maps can be represented via swim lanes where they flow across functional, organizational or team boundaries or they are represented based on the "overall flow" of a function or transaction. Both examples shown below serve the same purpose defining a process from start to finish.

Here is an example of a cross-functional swim lane process flow.

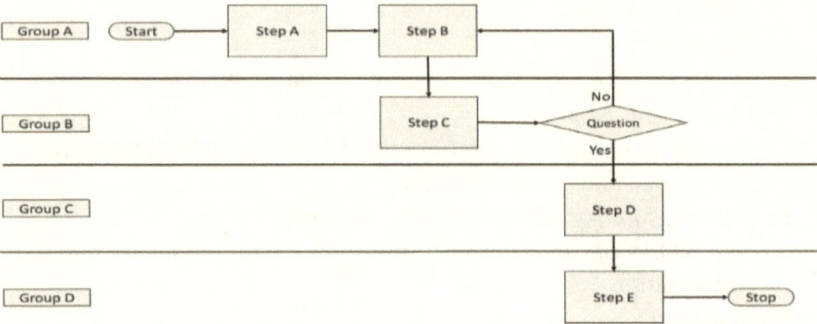

Here is an example a functional or transactional process flow. Note: This process flow contains the same data elements as the cross-functional swim lane process flow shown above.

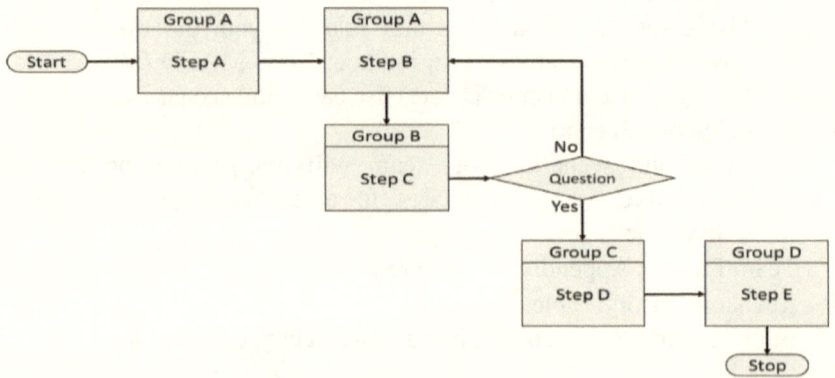

The Contract

The contract below represents an example of a contract or letter of intent between a team leader and an individual team member. It is a living document that can be changed based on the needs of the business or changing requirements when it comes to your individual team members.

Contract between the *<Team Leader Name>* and *<Team Member Name>*.

The provisions in this contract are as follows.

- The Team Leader promises to set the Team Member goals and expectations based on the job the Team Member possesses and is expected to perform.
- These expectations will be based on team member feedback and will represent and clearly define the high-level responsibilities and accountabilities of the Team Member as it relates to the Team Member's job. These expectations are as follows:
  o Expectation 1
  o Expectation 2
- This contract will define the high-level authority levels which the Team Member possesses. The authority levels for the Team Member are as follows:
  o Authority Level 1
  o Authority Level 2
- This contract will define the high-level items the team member is expected to satisfactorily achieve along with the positive key relationships the Team Member will build and maintain when dealing with other Team Members, internal and external partners, and / or your customer.

The Contract, (continued)

- This contract will define the Team Leader's role as it relates to the individual Team Member. This includes the Team Leader's role as a mentor, a coach and a teacher to the individual Team Member. When it is identified that the Team Member is weak in an area, the Team Leader will work with the Team Member to develop a lesson plan for improving the Team Member's abilities to perform their assigned work in order to successfully meet customer deliverables. The Team Leader's roles are as follows:
    - Team Leader's Role 1
    - Team Leader's Role 2
- Expanded Team Leader and Team Member details as they relate to this contract can be found in the team process and / or the Team Member's job guidelines or task list.
- Where modifications of the contract are required, it will be made based on the mutual consent of the Team Leader and the Team Member.

Signatures of the Team Leader and Team Member signify knowledge of and acceptance of this contract.

Team Leader Signature   *Team Member Signature*

Team Leader Printed Name & Title   Team Member Printed Name & Title

Date   *Date*

RACI Model

The RACI Model is a team matrix defining what a team member is responsible, accountable, consulting and informing for as it relates to a team member's job function or task.

RACI Chart		Legend	
		R: Responsible	
		A: Accountable	
		C: Consulting	
		I: Informing	
Project: Pre-Sales / Sales Process Phase 1			
Phase: Pre-Sales SDM			
Task ID & Task Name	Name 1	Name 2	Name 3
1 <Task>	R	A	C
2 <Task>	R, A	C	C, I
3 <Task>	R, A	C	I
4 <Task>	R	A	C
5 <Task>	R	A	C
6 <Task>	R	R, A	C
7 <Task>	I	R	A
Phase: Sales SDM			
Task ID & Task Name	Name 1	Name 2	Name 3
8 <Task>	R	A	C, I
9 <Task>	A	R	C
10 <Task>	R, A	C, I	R, A
11 <Task>	A	C	A
12 <Task>	R	A	C, I
13 <Task>	I	I	R, A
14 <Task>	R	A	C
Phase: Sales Engineering (SE) SDM			
Task ID & Task Name	Name 1	Name 2	Name 3
15 <Task>	R	A	C, I

Job Guidelines

Job guidelines will be inter-related to the team process and contain some of the same key elements. Your team member's job guidelines provide guidance for what your team members do as it relates to your process and your customer. Once again provide meaning, be SMART, use EEI and the 5 Whys (drill down) when defining your team member's job guidelines. The bullets below represent some key elements you can include (but are not all inclusive). Your institutional or team leadership will determine what is appropriate for your own team member's job guidelines.

- Team Mission Statement and Team Charter.
    - Summary of what your team does.
- Executive Summary, Goals and / or Team Objectives.
    - Provides an executive summary or overall goals for your team.
- Team Leadership Hierarchy.
    - A point-of-contact (POC) list of your management team to include, but not limited to: Vice Presidents, Directors, Managers, Supervisors and / or Team Leads.
- RACI Model and Team Roles and Responsibilities.
    - Responsible, Accountable, Consulting and Informing Model of your team. In addition to the RACI Model (matrix), defined team roles and responsibilities provided to your customer to let your customer know who does what when it comes to the customer deliverable along with any job or positional boundaries that may be present for your team member.
- Authority Levels for the team member.
    - Authority levels when it comes to making key decisions as they relate to your customer. Can be in written or table format.
- Team Process Map and Narrative.
    - A process map and narrative of your team process. Team titles can be part of the process map and narrative. The process narrative is used to further define a step within the process map where there may be a text-count or size limitation in its graphical representation.

Job Guidelines, (continued)

- Team Member Customer Deliverables.
  - All defined (in-scope) customer deliverables for the team member. Helps to set the job or positional boundaries that may be present for your team member.
- Team Member Non-Deliverables.
  - Items that are considered out-of-scope to your team member as it relates to your customer or your customer deliverables. Helps to set the job or positional boundaries that may be present for your team member.
- Team Member Constraints, Dependencies, Assumptions and / or Business Rules (where known).
  - Individual sub-bullets defining the constraints, dependencies, assumptions and / or business rules for the team member that may prevent successful customer delivery. Can be system or human factors related.
    - Constraints.
    - Dependencies.
    - Assumptions.
    - Business Rules.
- Team Environment.
  - Environmental factors that can impact your team member. Can be:
    - Operational.
    - Organizational.
    - System related.
- Team Reporting Requirements.
  - All reporting requirements and their delivery frequency as it relates to the team process and your customer.
- Signatures and Approvals.
  - Who signs what and their approval levels (can be defined by scope size and / or budget size).
- Revision History Table.
  - Used for version control and acts as a change history log.

Task List Option

Task lists are used to summarize job functions or tasks that are considered less critical and secondary in nature vs. a team member's primary or regular job functions or tasks.

Task List

Task and Sub-Task Name			
Task: Define Requirements	Assigned To:	When Due:	Date Completed:
Sub-Task: AS-IS Process	Name 1	5/1/2016	5/1/2016
Sub-Task: TO-BE Process	Name 1	5/2/2016	5/2/2016
Sub-Task: Business Process	Name 1	5/2/2016	5/2/2016
Sub-Task: System Process	Name 2	5/3/2016	In Progress
Sub-Task: KPI / GAP Analysis	Name ½	5/4-11/2016	
Task and Sub-Task Name			
Task: Code and Unit / System / Integration Test	Assigned To:	When Due:	Date Completed:
Sub-Task: Table Hierarchy	Name 3	5/5/2016	
Sub-Task: Code Definition	Name 3	5/5/2016	
Sub-Task: Coding	Name 3	5/6-7/2016	
Sub-Task: Unit Test	Name 3	5/8/2016	
Sub-Task: System Test	Name 4	5/9/2016	
Sub-Task: Integration Test	Name 4	5/10-11/2016	
Sub-Task: Debug / Break Fix	Name 3	5/8-11/2016	

Process Improvement Plan (Problem Statement or Charter)

This table represents a problem statement your team can use when it comes time to address process improvement. In it, you have your problem statement, the business impact, the goal statement, what is in-scope and out-of-scope, high-level project plan dates and your team members. Note: The process improvement plan structure is no different than that of a project or a team charter with the exception that the SSBOK and their DMAIC process groups are used below in place of the project phases.

PROBLEM STATEMENT or CHARTER	BUSINESS IMPACT
What is the specific problem that needs to be addressed? • Addresses the specific problem using EEI, SMART and The 5 Whys techniques. Not intended to point blame on any one person, organization or institution	What are the business impacts? • Addresses the impacts to the team, the institution, and / or the business
GOAL STATEMENT	**PROJECT SCOPE**
Defines the ultimate goal to be reached by addressing the problem • *Example* - Cut cycle time • *Example* - Meet SLA	Defines what is in-scope and what is out-of-scope • In-scope requirements • Out-of-scope requirements
PROCESS IMPROVEMENT PROJECT PLAN DATES	**TEAM SELECTION**
Project: Start Date to Anticipated Finish Date Define Task: Start Date to Anticipated Finish Date Measure Task: Start Date to Anticipated Finish Date Analyze Task: Start Date to Anticipated Finish Date Improve Task: Start Date to Anticipated Finish Date Control Task: Start Date to Anticipated Finish Date (Customer Expected completion is <Date>) Note: To be effective, Process Improvement projects should not be set with an end-date in mind, but should be based on the satisfactory project delivery and buy-in from the Project Sponsor and the Project Champion after the process improvement plan has been successfully completed. Phase dates can overlap. These dates must be realistic and achievable.	Project Sponsor: <Name> Project Champion: (Name> Project Manager: <Name> Project Team Members: <Names>

Brainstorming, Affinity Diagram, Nominal Group Technique, Inter-relational Digraph, Data Collection and GAP Analysis

For new ideas you may come up with or for every problem you may encounter, there are tools and processes you can use from which you can start your process or problem definition. These tools and processes are used to generate new ideas or to define the root cause to an existing problem. Below is a summary list of steps you can perform which includes the following:

- Brainstorming – Gathering a list of ideas without criticism.
- Affinity Diagram – Taking a list of ideas and organizing or grouping them in categories or buckets.
- Nominal Group Technique – Taking a list of ideas and prioritizing them 1 to 5.
- Inter-relational Digraph – Taking a list of ideas and determining which idea has more influence over another idea starting with the least influential idea and working towards the most influential idea. Connecting the related ideas together with arrows.
- Data Collection and GAP Analysis – Comparing the AS-IS process with the future TO-BE process and running GAP analysis against the two.

RCA – Fault Tree Diagram and The 5 Whys

The diagram provided here represents a simplified version of a fault tree diagram which is used when conducting The 5 Whys question and answer session. At the top, you list the problem statement and from there you drill down until you reach the actual root cause. The answer and question session can go through 5 levels or can end at very first level based on its answer as it relates to the actual root cause.

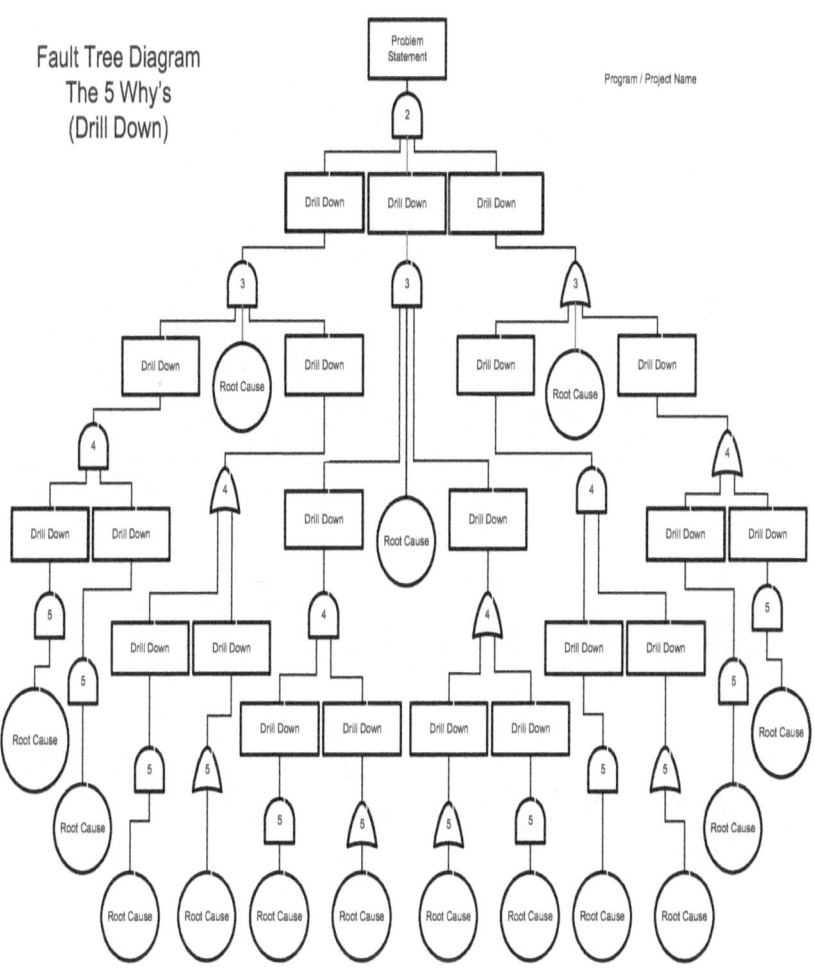

RCA – Cause and Effect Diagram, Isakawa Diagram or Fishbone Diagram (7Ms) (ASQ Seven Tools of Quality)

Cause and effect diagram, Isakawa diagram or fishbone diagram helps breakdown a problem into categories and sub-categories. The 7M categories are Mother Nature, Materials, Methods, Manpower, Measurement, Machines and Management.

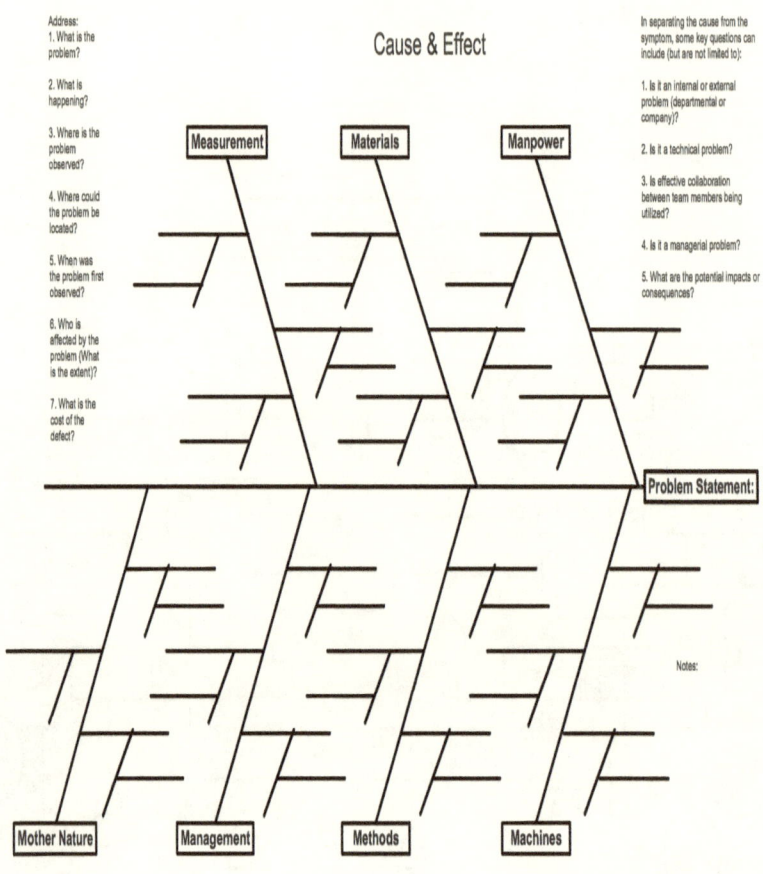

RCA – Pareto Chart (ASQ Seven Tools of Quality)

When using pareto charts, you will discover that typically 80% of your problems can be addressed in the top 20% of your defects. Addressing the top 3 defects can also very beneficial to team success if the top 20% of the defects do not fit your process improvement criteria or needs.

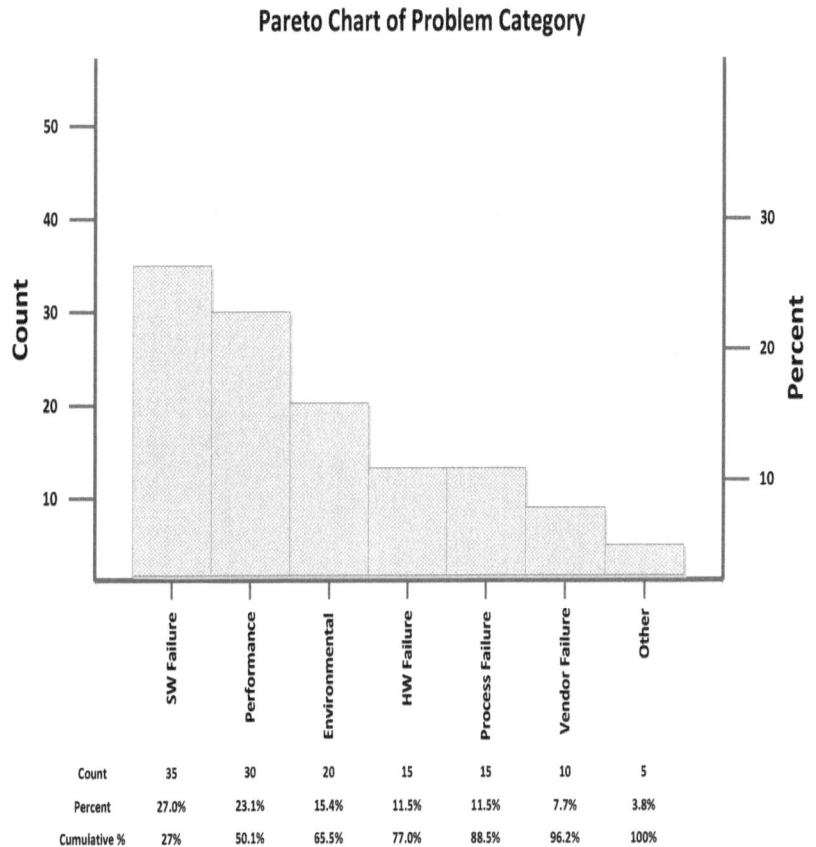

Pareto Chart of Problem Category

	SW Failure	Performance	Environmental	HW Failure	Process Failure	Vendor Failure	Other
Count	35	30	20	15	15	10	5
Percent	27.0%	23.1%	15.4%	11.5%	11.5%	7.7%	3.8%
Cumulative %	27%	50.1%	65.5%	77.0%	88.5%	96.2%	100%

Control Chart (ASQ Seven Tools of Quality)

Control charts are excellent for measuring a process or process "velocity" over time. Within the control chart you will define the upper and lower control limits based on the median or the mean. Anything beyond these control limits should be considered out of specification or tolerance to the overall process and should be addressed and analyzed via a process improvement plan.

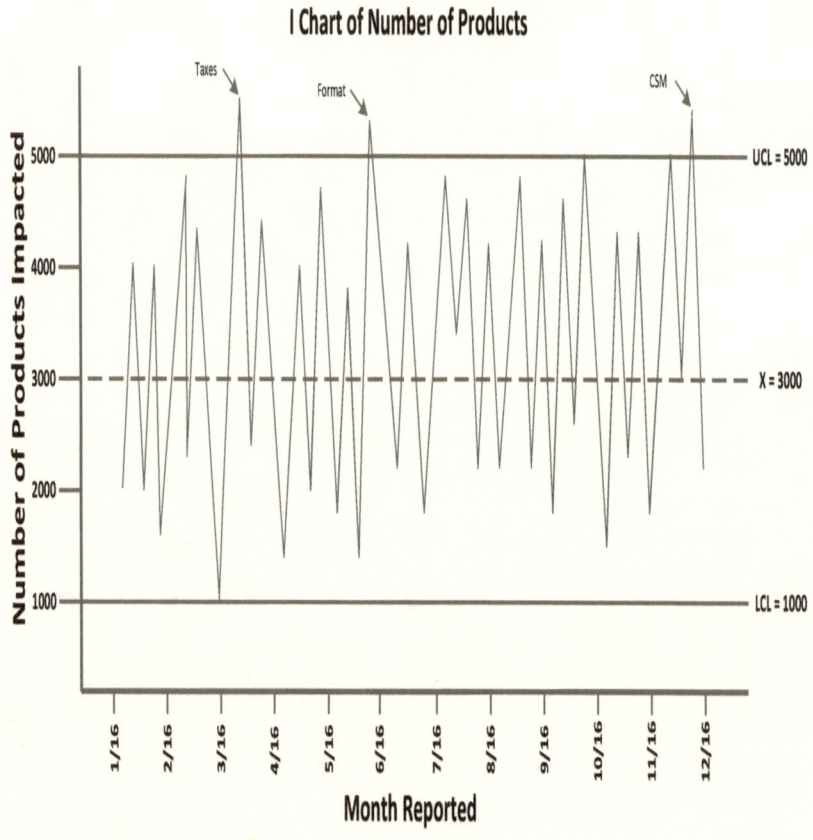

Dashboard and Benchmarking

Dashboards provide you quick summary metrics of the team's performance. They can also be used to benchmark your team's performance against others. They are typically weekly to bi-weekly in nature but can be over whatever time period the team desires (monthly, quarterly, etc.).

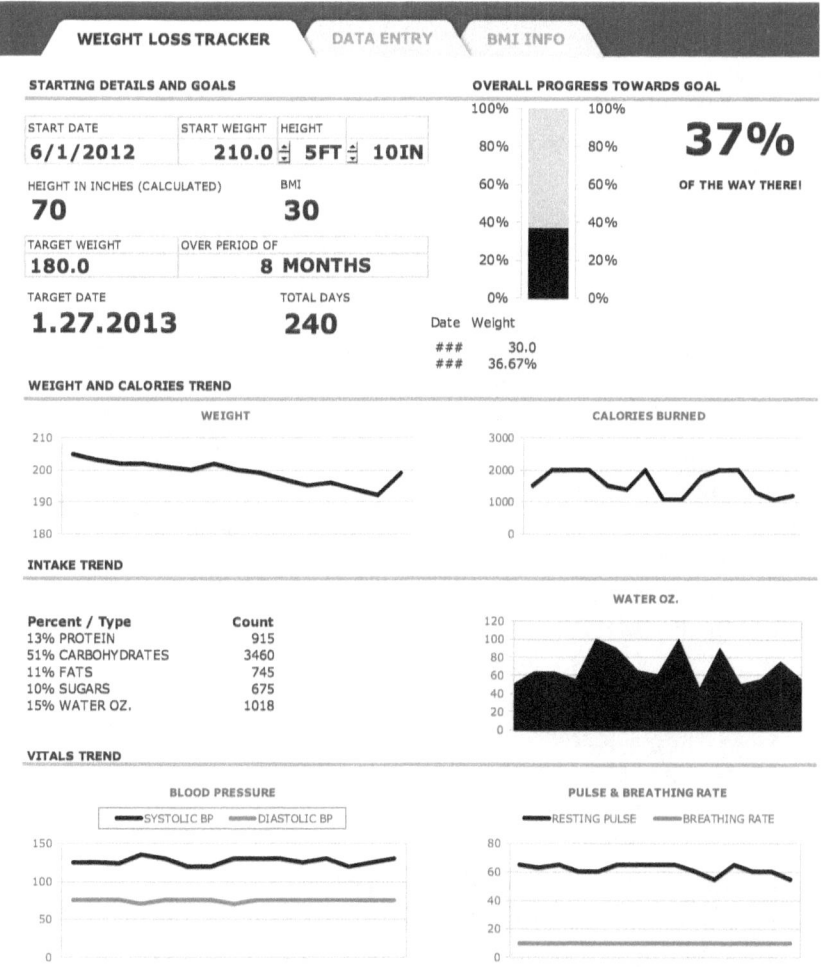

Appendix B – References

Appendix B references the sources from which some of this book's material comes from. Some of these references include some of the original Power motivation authors and their respective books. It is highly recommended that you get a copy of their books and learn from them no different than what you have learned from reading this book.

- Agile Manifesto Twelve Principles, (http://agilemanifesto.org)
  - Principles – Work together daily; Motivated individuals; Self-organizing teams and team reflection
- AMC
  - *Mad Men's episode Waterloo*, "A Leader is loyal to his team"
  - *Mad Men's episode The Summer Man*, Aesop's fable of the Sun and the Wind
- Erika Andersen, *21 Quotes from Henry Ford on Business, Leadership and Life,* (Forbes Magazine, May 13, 2013)
  - Quotes on Vision, mistakes and learning
- T. M. Kubiak and Donald W. Benbow, *The Certified Six Sigma Black Belt Handbook, Second Edition,* (ASQ Quality Press, 2009) (Reprinted with permission from the American Society for Quality, Quality Press © 2009 ASQ, www.asq.org, February 11, 2016)
  - Strategic and Tactical Planning
  - 3 Categories of Planning
  - Quality Management and the Kaizen
  - 1st, 2nd, and 3rd Law of Lean Six Sigma
  - Brainstorming
  - Affinity Diagram
  - Nominal Group Technique
  - Inter-relational Digraph
  - Flowcharting
  - Data Collection and GAP Analysis
  - Root Cause Analysis (RCA)
  - Fault Tree Diagram
  - The 5 Whys
  - Cause and Effect Diagram
  - Pareto Chart

- Control Chart
- Dashboard and Benchmarking
- Dr. Robert J. Bies, Georgetown University, Seminar: *Seeking the Creative Edge through Innovation*, September 23, 2015; (Reprinted with permission from Dr. Bies, 9/23/2015)
  - Anticipation and Adaptation
  - Will Rogers quote on The right track
  - Focus on your mission when planning
  - Michelangelo quote on Taking aim
  - Charles Kettering quote on Always done it this way
  - G.K. Chesterton quote on Solution to a problem
  - Voice and Listen
  - Jack Welch quote on Culture
  - Warren Buffet quote on Trust
  - The 4 C's
  - Cultivate and Connect
  - Margaret Mead quote on Commitment
  - Peter Drucker quote on Commitment
  - Michael Jordan quote on Talent wins games
  - David Starr Jordan quote on Wisdom, skill and virtue
  - Steve Jobs quote on Innovation
  - Linus Paulding quote on Brainstorming
  - Benchmarking
- brainyquote.com
  - Vince Lombardi quote on Individual commitment
  - John Wooden quote on Details
  - Tony Robbins quote on Turning the invisible to visible
  - Louis Pasteur quote on Fortune
  - Bo Jackson quote on Goals
  - President Dwight D Eisenhower quote on Motivation
  - President Theodore Roosevelt quote on Complaining
  - President John F. Kennedy quote on Leadership and learning
  - Walt Disney quote on Dreaming
- CBS
  - *Quicken Loans National Golf Tournament*, Victory interview with Kyle Stanley, Focus on the process, July 2, 2017

- *60 Minutes Interview, Feeding Puerto Rico*, Interview with Chef Jose Andres, November 27, 2017
- *60 Minutes Interview, Theo and Joe*, Interview with Joe Maddon and Theo Epstein, Chicago Cubs, May 7, 2017
- *Cheers' episode A Bar is Born*, Quote on Courage
- Ram Charan, Dominic Barton and Dennis Carey, *Talent Wins: The New Playbook for putting People First*, (Harvard Business Review Press, 2018)
  - Susan Peters quote on Positive coaching
  - Investments in training
  - Talent is the value creator
  - Agile companies like Facebook
- Stephen Covey, *The 7 Habits of Highly Effective People: Powerful Lessons in Personal Change*, (Simon & Schuster, Anniversary Edition, 2013)
  - Quote on Fundamental principles
  - Habit 2, Begin with the end in mind
  - Quote on Trust
  - Quote on Listening
  - Quote on Power
  - Quote Effective leadership and character
  - Peter Drucker and Warren Bennis quote on Management and leadership
  - Albert Einstein quote on Problem solving
  - Habit 6, Synergize
  - Aristotle quote on Habits
  - Quote on Habits defined (Knowledge, Skill and Desire)
  - Habit 1, Be proactive and values
  - Quote on Team mission statement
- Mitch Ditkoff, *50 Awesome Quotes on Risk Taking*, (huffingtonpost.com, November 10, 2016)
  - Rear Admiral Grace Hopper quote on "If it is a good idea…"
  - Wayne Gretzky quote on 100%
  - Frederick Wilcox quote on Progress
  - President Jimmy Carter quote on "Going out on a limb…"
- Eileen Forrester, Brandon L. Buteau and Sandy Schum, *CMMI for Service, Guidelines for Superior Service, CMMI-SVC Version 1.2*, (Addison-Wesley, Pearson Education, Inc., 2010)

- Process Area Categories
- Generic Goals and Practices; Capability and Maturity Levels
- Benjamin Franklin quotes
  - Quote on Energy and persistence
  - Quote on Those that fail to plan
  - Quote on Prevention
- Jeffrey Gitomer, *The Little RED Book of Selling*, (Bard Press, 2005)
  - Quote on Respect and credibility lead to trust
  - 1st Principle for Selling
- Patrick Lencioni, *The Five Dysfunctions of a Team*, (Jossey-Bass, 2002)
  - Quote on Trust
  - Quote and Steps for a cohesive team
- LinkedIn.com
  - General Colin Powell quote on Leadership, Forbes@100
  - Jack and Suzy Welch, *Are Leaders Born or Made? Here's What's Coachable — and What's Definitely Not*, Five Essential Traits to Leadership
  - Rocky Thurston, *The Epitome of Teamwork*, May 2, 2017
  - Howard Schultz quote on Commitment and purpose, Forbes@100
- Abraham Maslow, *A Theory of Human Motivation*, (Martino Publishing, 2013)
  - Hierarchy of Human Needs
  - Quote on Goals
  - Quote on Organized vs. unorganized world
  - Quote on A Healthy Man
- From *How Successful People Lead: Taking your Influence to the Next Level* by John C. Maxwell, copyright © 2013. (Reprinted by permission of Center Street an imprint of Hachette Book Group, Inc.)
  - Quote on Investing in your people
  - Quote on Invitation to lead
  - Quote on Leadership and the organization's vision
  - Quote on the Hallmarks of successful leadership
  - Quote on Knowing your own strengths and weaknesses
- David McClelland, *Human Motivation*, (Cambridge University Press, 1987)

- Motivation and PAA
- Quote on Motives drive, orient and select behavior
- Merriam-Webster's on-line dictionary
  - Power
  - Responsibility
  - Accountability
  - Authority
  - Motivation
  - Achievement
  - Affiliation
  - People
  - Talent
  - Experience
  - Technique
- National Broadcast Company
  - *NFL Thursday Night Football*, Tony Dungy quote on Chuck Noll and team fundamentals (December 1, 2016)
  - RBC Canadian Open Commercial quote on Having the right people behind you
- Paramount Pictures
  - *Coach Carter*, Team Member Contract
  - *Braveheart*, Men follow courage
  - *The Godfather*, "It's just business"
- General George S. Patton; Patton Museum; Ft. Knox, Ky
  - Quote on Leadership
  - Quote on Risk
  - Quote on Ingenuity
- Babe Ruth, (baberuth.com)
  - Quote on Fear of striking out
  - Quote on Team success
- Edgar H. Schein, *Organizational Culture and Leadership*, (John Wiley & Sons, Inc., 4th Edition, 2010)
  - Quote on Culture and leadership
  - Quote on Character and culture
- Simon Sinek Quotes,
  - Quote on Dreaming
  - Quote on Team trust

- Jeff Shore, *These 10 Peter Drucker Quotes may Change the World*, (Entrepreneur.com on-line article)
  - Quote on Long range planning and measuring
  - Quote on Meetings
- USA Today, *30 of Muhammad Ali's best quotes*, June 5, 2016
  - Quote on Bragging (confidence)
  - Quote on Courage
  - Quote on Imagination
- Warner Brother Pictures
  - *Caddy Shack*, "See your future, Be your future"
  - *Storks*, "Make a plan, stick to the plan, always deliver"
  - *The Replacements*, "Lead your team, earn their respect"
- 20th Century Fox
  - *Master and Commander, The Far Side of the World*, "Respect comes from strength and discipline"
  - *TAPS*, "The loyalty of men is always hard earned"
  - *Wall Street*, "The most valuable Commodity is Information"
  - *The Hustler*, "It is not enough that you just have talent, you have to have character too"
- Abbott and Costello, *Who's on 1st*
- President John Adams quote on Problems and opportunities
- Amy Carpenter Aquino, *Eye to Eye with Ebola, Lessons in safety and unity in treating 4 US patients*, SOP and Accountability, (ENA Connection magazine, Vol. 39, Issue 5, May 2015)
- Ken Blanchard and Spencer Johnson, *The New One Minute Manager*, "Feedback is the breakfast of champions", (William Morrow, 2015)
- Sir Richard Branson quote on Train people well
- Buena Vista Pictures, *Remember the Titans*, "Attitude reflects leadership"
- Dale Carnegie, *How to Win Friends and Influence People*, Principle # 1, (Pocket Books, 1981)
- General Wesley Clark quote on talent, (Pinterest.com)
- Columbia Pictures, *The Bridge on the River Kwai* and Warner Brother Pictures, *The Shining*, "All work and no play makes Jack a very dull boy"
- Comedy Central, *South Park*, Cartman, "Respect my Authoritah!"
- EA Sports, *Madden 11*, Drew Brees, Quote on Winning

- Albert Einstein quote on Imagination
- Geico Insurance Commercial quote on Greatness
- Daniel Goleman, Richard Boyatzis and Annie McKee, *Primal Leadership: Learning to Lead with Emotional Intelligence*, Quote on Responsibility and the state of mind, (Harvard Business Review Press, 2013)
- Jeff Haden, Article on Google leadership, (Inc.com)
- Frederic Herzburg, Bernard Mausner and Barbara Bloch Snyderman, *The Motivation to Work*, Theory of Hygiene Factors, (Transaction Publishers, 1993)
- Conn and Hal Iggulden, *The Dangerous Book for Boys*, Douglas Bader quote on Rules and guidance (HarperCollins Publishers, 2006)
- isixsigma.com, takt time definition
- Coach Tom Izzo, Michigan State University Basketball Program, Active Listening, "Learn to listen, Listen to learn"
- Geoffrey James, *Top 10 Motivational books of all time*, Norman Vincent Peale quote on Action, (inc.com, March 22, 2013)
- Steve Jobs quote on Courage, heart & intuition, and passion.
- Michael Jordan quote on "I have failed many times…"
- Eugene Kim, *Business Leaders explain why they love Amazon CEO Jeff Bezos' annual letter so much*, Long-term thinking, (CNBC Tech, April 19, 2018)
- Pat Matson Knapp, HOW Business Columnist interview with Peter Block on Leading the Way, (HOW, April 2005)
- Latin Proverb, "Fortune favors the bold"
- *President Abraham Lincoln's Temperance speech*, February 22, 1842, Quote on persuasion
- Microsoft Surface Commercial and collaboration quote
- Microsoft templates, Dashboard
- Netflix Pictures, *War Machine*, Quote on Talent; (May 26, 2017)
- New Line Cinema, *Lord of the Rings Trilogy*, Gandalf the Gray and Aragon
- Orion Pictures, *Hoosiers*, Four pass offense
- Shane Parrish, *What Warren Buffet would say about your stressful work environment*, Environments, (Farnam Street on-line article)
- PBS, Ken Burn's *The Civil War*, Episode 1, Quote on President Abraham Lincoln and Talent
- President Franklin D. Roosevelt quote on "Fear…"

- President Theodore Roosevelt quote on "The difference between a leader and a boss…"
- Emmitt Smith quote on Goals and dreams
- Sun Tzu quote on Every battle is won
- Justin Thomas quote on "See it, don't waver…" (Golf Digest, Oct. 2017)
- President Harry S. Truman quote on "The Buck stops here"
- Bruce Tuckman, *Forming, Storming, Norming, Performing*
- Mark Twain quote on "Getting started…"
- Anthony Ulwick, *Best Practice: Uncovering Unmet Customer Needs*, Job Mapping, (MarketingJournal.org, June 17, 2016)
- Universal Pictures, *Seabiscuit*, Emily Dickinson poem "We never know how high we are…"
- Various internet website quotes for President Abraham Lincoln and Peter Drucker, "The best way to predict the future is to create it"
- Minnesota Governor Jesse Ventura quote on "Live the dream…"
- Coach Bill Walsh quote on motivated winners
- William "Bill" Walton, *The New Bottom Line*, Short Course in Human Relations, (Publisher unknown, book out of print)
- H.G. Wells quote on the future
- Oscar Wilde Quote on Experience is the one thing you can't get for nothing, (PosterEnvy, Amazon.com)

www.ingramcontent.com/pod-product-compliance
Lightning Source LLC
Chambersburg PA
CBHW032021170526
45157CB00002B/799